Training in Environmental Management – Industry and Sustainability

Part 1

Corporate Environmental and Resource Management and Educational Requirements

EF/96/17/EN

BIOGRAPHICAL SKETCHES OF AUTHORS

JOHN P. ULHØI is Associate Professor at the Aarhus School of Business, Denmark (Department of Organisation and Management). He has a Master's degree in Urban and Regional Planning and a PhD in Business Administration. He has research and teaching experience in the fields of Strategic Management, Technology Management, Technology Assessment and Corporate Greening and has published several papers in these areas. He is a reviewer for four international journals and has organised and chaired sessions at international conferences.

HENNING MADSEN is Associate Professor at the Aarhus School of Business, Denmark (Department of Information Science). He received his Master's degree in Mathematical Economics from the University of Aarhus and a PhD in Business Economics from the Aarhus School of Business. He has chaired sessions at several international conferences and acted as referee as well. His current research interests include Technological Forecasting and Forecasting in Environmental Analyses.

PÁLL M. RIKHARDSSON is a research assistant at the Aarhus School of Business, Denmark (Department of Organisation and Management). He has a Master's degree in Economics from the University of Reykjavik and a Master's degree in Business Administration from the Aarhus School of Business. His current research interests include Strategic Environmental Management, Environmental Performance Measurement and Environmental Reporting.

Training in Environmental Management – Industry and Sustainability

PART 1

Corporate Environmental and Resource Management and Educational Requirements

by

John P. Ulhøi
Henning Madsen
Páll M. Rikhardsson
The Aarhus School of Business

European Foundation
for the Improvement of Living and Working Conditions
Loughlinstown, Dublin 18, Ireland
Tel: +353 1 282 6888   Fax: +353 1 282 6456

Cataloguing data can be found at the end of this publication

Luxembourg: Office for Official Publications of the European Communities, 1996

ISBN 92-827-6927-5

© European Foundation for the Improvement of Living and Working Conditions, 1996

For rights of translation or reproduction, applications should be made to the Director, European Foundation for the Improvement of Living and Working Conditions, Loughlinstown, Dublin 18, Ireland.

Printed in Ireland

ACKNOWLEDGEMENTS

This study was carried out by a research team at the Aarhus School of Business consisting of:

Associate Professor John Parm Ulhøi, PhD, Department of Organisation and Management,
Associate Professor Henning Madsen, PhD, Department of Information Sciences,
Research Assistant Páll Melsted Rikhardsson, MSc,
Project Assistant Christine S. Sundstrup, BA, and
Project Secretary Steve Churchill, BSc.

The team would like to thank all contacts in companies and educational institutions who responded to the requests for information and interviews.

PREFACE

Managerial training and higher education have long been recognised as essential ingredients of improved environmental and resource management and, hence, as a vital basis for progress towards sustainable development. The suggestion for an international programme on environmental education dates back as far as 1972 when it was brought forward at the United Nations' Stockholm Conference on the Human Environment. Twenty years later, at the United Nations' Conference on Environment and Development in Rio, a whole chapter of Agenda 21 was devoted to a plan of action for sustainable development which called for national strategies for environmental education.

At the EU level the starting point for joint action in this area was Council Resolution on Environmental Education of 29 May 1988. Since then, a considerable number of initiatives have been undertaken, both nationally and by the EU institutions, covering primary and secondary education as well as professional education and training. In the context of this report, it is worth noting that the Commission in recognition of the fundamental role of education and training in promoting sustainable development has integrated environment-related courses and projects in its own education and training programmes, notably COMETT, ERASMUS, PETRA, EUROTECHNET, FORCE and TEMPUS. The environmental component was also reinforced when the European Parliament and the Council, in March 1995, adopted the SOCRATES Programme, amalgamating and extending the ERASMUS and LINGUA Programmes. In addition, an EU Study Guide on University Environment Courses was published, in 1993, providing an analysis of the extent to which environmental courses have been integrated in third-level institutions, and at the same time a "European Master's Degree in Environmental Management" was established at nine universities in the Union. Moreover, the Commission has in recent years co-financed a number of training courses, seminars and workshops for planners, accountants and auditors.

The Foundation's work on environment-related education and training issues had until 1993 included two studies: one on education and training relating to hazardous waste (1988-1989) and one on education and training of personnel concerned with environmental issues relating to industry. The latter highlighted the training needs of SMEs, in particular, and was the first stage of a still ongoing project (the firm and the environment) examining the characteristics and the potential of locally and regionally based cooperation initiatives and networks involving firms, public authorities, the social partners, industrial federations, etc., in bringing about improvements in the environmental performance of smaller enterprises. The findings of this work were presented at a European Round Table on "Industry, Social Dialogue and Sustainability", 1-2 December 1992 in Rome, where it was proposed that the Foundation as part of its activities include a series of studies on training in environmental management in its four-year programme 1993-1996. This proposal was endorsed by the Administrative Board of the Foundation and supported by the services of the Commission (Directorate-General XI). Thus, the Fifth Environmental Policy and Action Programme points to the crucial role of industry in the present and future efforts towards achieving sustainable development and to the need for involving it more actively in this process, so as to ensure the improved resource management and high environmental standards required in the future. An important element in these endeavours is the creation of a new form of awareness throughout industry based on sound environmental performance as a challenge, which can not only be used to reduce production costs, but can also serve as an instrument for further development and expansion in a market becoming increasingly competitive and demanding "green" products. In fact, a number of companies have already, with various degrees of success, started to meet this challenge introducing new and often innovative and dynamic corporate strategies merging economic/business and environmental considerations, and many more are considering it. This process of change, however, calls for new skills at all levels of the firm, not least among managers, and hence education and training provision will have to be adapted to these requirements in a close cooperation between the parties concerned, notably industry and educational establishments. An example of an initiative in this respect is the EU Programme for Education and Training in Technology (COMETT) which was actually launched with the purpose of creating a network of University – Enterprise Training Partnerships (UETPs).

It was on these grounds that the Foundation felt that there was an urgent need for undertaking a project focusing on the future educational and training requirements brought about by the introduction of new corporate environmental and resource management strategies as part of the move towards sustainable development. For practical and financial reasons the project was divided into three stages, each of them covering one of the three groups primarily involved in the implementation of the new strategies, i.e.

- Managers with responsibility for the development of industrial and business strategies (typically top management and high-level middle management);
- categories of (mostly technical) middle management; and
- categories of lower management and workers.

The first stage, the TEM-1 Project, which is the subject of this report, was carried out in 1993-1994 and looks into corporate environmental and resource management introduced in recent years in a number of European companies and the educational and training provision which is and will be required in relation to existing and future managers concerned with developing integrated and environment-related industrial and business strategies. This part of the project also had to provide the basis of the following stages in two respects. First, it was clear that, in order to fully understand and identify the educational requirements of the three above-mentioned groups, special attention would have to be paid to the corporate managerial aspects, notably in some of the EU's leading companies. Second, as there appeared to be some confusion in the use of the concept of sustainable development, an extensive literature review was undertaken, as a first step, with the aim of arriving at an operational definition of corporate sustainability. Furthermore, information was obtained from a large panel of researchers and other experts in this area in order to identify for further analysis a sample of companies and institutions of higher education at the centre of the greening process of change.

This enabled the Contractor, the Department of Organisation and Management of the Aarhus School of Business, to focus on the key issues in a more structured way. The report describes and analyses the existing practices of industrial environmental management, existing higher education and training of future managers who are likely to be involved in company policies regarding environmental issues, and the inadequacies of and mismatches between providers and users of higher management education. It also points to the need for further information so as to provide a better understanding of what is, actually, happening, and it discusses some of the major obstacles to improvements of the present situation as well as potential solutions which may contribute to closing, at least, part of the gap identified between the higher management education provision and the needs of industry.

The report was discussed at a meeting on 30 March 1995 in Brussels to enable representatives of the employers, trade unions, governments and the European Commission – the constituent bodies of the Foundation's Administrative Board – to evaluate the findings of the research. The participants stressed the value and quality of the work and made some suggestions, notably regarding the presentation, which have been taken into account in the preparation of the final report. They referred to the great importance of environmental education and training as it provided relevant qualifications and offered employment opportunities when it was added on to or combined with other subjects. On the other hand, as a main subject on its own environmental studies offered little or no employment prospect. The participants also felt that it was essential that a close connection between environmental education and training and the requirements of the labour market be ensured and that this connection be considered in the context of the efforts towards combining growth and sustainable development. Hence, educational systems would increasingly have to be adapted to future requirements which so far had usually not been the case, and the Foundation might have a role in this respect. In addition, it would be necessary to find a balance in the educational system between generalists and specialists as both categories were needed in the labour market. At present, it appeared that generalists with some degree of specialisation were the more successful. Moreover, it was mentioned that, although it was generally agreed that a strengthening of environmental training of workers was required (it is specifically mentioned in the Environmental Management and Audit Scheme, EMAS), the attitude of top management in this respect and to the involvement of workers in environmental issues was far from clear. There were, however, positive examples of a cooperation between trade unions and progressive industrialists in this respect.

In conclusion, the representatives agreed that the Foundation should, gradually, enlarge its field of investigation in this area through a cooperation with CEDEFOP and other relevant bodies and that other sectors than industry, e.g. local authorities, may have to be covered as their role and activities relating to the environment are likely to have implications for environmental training requirements. The suggestion was made that the Foundation may consider organising a conference on environmental education and training once its studies are more advanced.

The second part of the project was undertaken in 1995. It focuses on the educational and training requirements of categories of lower management and workers in the light of the new corporate environment-related strategies and is expected to be completed in the near future. It will be followed up, in 1996, by a third study covering categories of mostly technical middle management and, in 1997, by a consolidated report bringing together the findings of the whole project.

The work in this area is part of the Foundation's programme on socio-economic aspects of the environment/sustainable development 1993-1996. In this programme priority has been given to the situation of industry and the business sector at large in the context of the move towards sustainability and the challenge and potential which the latter means in terms of future developments, the need for new support structures and cooperation schemes for SMEs, job creation, cleaner production processes and products, the role of the cooperation between the social partners, and, obviously, education and training. Although much attention has been paid to issues of particular importance to SMEs, some of which are, at the moment, faced with major environmental and financial problems, the typical education and training requirements of these enterprises are not dealt with explicitly in the present four-year programme, but they are likely to be included in the next one 1997-2000.

Jørn Pedersen
Research Manager
Coordinator,
Environment/Sustainable Development Programme

CONTENTS

EXECUTIVE SUMMARY		xxiii
1.0 INTRODUCTION AND BACKGROUND		1
1.1	Introduction to the Concept of Sustainability	1
	1.1.1 The Road to Sustainable Development	4
1.2	The European Union's Concept of Sustainability	7
1.3	Sustainability - a Business Issue	9
	1.3.1 Conclusion	16
1.4	Corporate Greening and Management Education	16
1.5	Research Objectives and Definition of Terms	20
	1.5.1 General issues	20
	1.5.2 Specific issues	21
1.6	Method of Approach	21
	1.6.1 Objectives of the data collection	21
	1.6.2 Structure of the data collection	21
	1.6.3 Sample selection	22
	1.6.4 The data collection	23
	1.6.5 Analysing the data	30
2.0 CORPORATE ENVIRONMENTAL AND RESOURCE MANAGEMENT: STATE OF THE ART		33
2.1	Corporate Environmental Practices	33
	2.1.1 General information	33
	2.1.2 Company profiles	33
	2.1.3 Information about the respondents	36
	2.1.4 Drivers of environmental management	37

2.1.5	Main environmental problems	38
2.1.6	Values and objectives expressed in corporate and/or environmental policy	39
2.1.7	Company environmental philosophy	45
2.1.8	Environmental management systems and certification	46
2.1.9	The organisational approach to environmental issu	49
2.1.10	Operational goals and initiatives	51
2.1.11	Environmental management tools and methods	53
2.1.12	Financial and accounting issues	58
2.1.13	HRM and the environment	58
2.1.14	Environmental management educational requirements	62
2.1.15	Marketing, advertising, and competition	64
2.1.16	Technology and R&D	65
2.1.17	Relations and/or communications with external stakeholders	65
2.1.18	The use of external consultants	68
2.1.19	Future expectations	68
2.1.20	Sustainability issues	72
2.1.21	Other observations	73
2.2	Conclusion: Characteristics of Existing Environmental Management Practices	74

3.0 EXAMPLES OF ENVIRONMENTAL MANAGEMENT PRACTICES — 79

3.1	Introduction	79
3.2	Examples of environmental management responses	79
3.2.1	Example1: Managerial and organisational approaches to corporate environmental improvement	79
3.2.2	Example 2: Corporate responsibility and environmental education requirements	83
3.2.3	Example 3: Practising general environmental management	86
3.2.4	Example 4: Communicating environmental performance	89

4.0 ENVIRONMENTAL MANAGEMENT EDUCATION AND TRAINING INITIATIVES: STATE OF THE ART — 93

4.1	Training in Environmental Management	93
4.1.1	Institutions of higher education	93

4.1.2	The respondents	94
4.1.3	Drivers of sustainability in higher education	94
4.1.4	Environmental courses offered	96
4.1.5	Teaching approaches and materials	105
4.1.6	The role of EM educators and educational institutions	106
4.1.7	The ideal environmental education	107
4.1.8	Barriers to the greening of curricula	107
4.1.9	Relations with business	108
4.1.10	Current and future research activities	109
4.1.11	General expectations for the future	111
4.1.12	Other observations	111
4.2	Conclusion: Characteristics of Existing Management Education	112

5.0 EXAMPLES OF ENVIRONMENTAL MANAGEMENT EDUCATION AND TRAINING INITIATIVES 117

5.1	Introduction	117
5.2	Examples	117
5.2.1	Example 1: Training interdisciplinary environmental consultants	117
5.2.2	Example 2: Developing an environmental MBA programme	120
5.2.3	Example 3: Educating environmental business economists	123

6.0 CONCLUSIONS AND FUTURE ACTIONS AND ACTIVITIES 127

6.1	The Present and Future Role of Industrial Leaders and Self-Regulation	127
6.2	General Conclusions for Industry	130
6.3	The Present and Future Role of Institutions of Higher Education	136
6.4	General Conclusions for Educational Institutions	138
6.5	Future Managerial and Educational Needs	145
6.6	Future research	146

ANNEXES

Annex 1:	References	149
Annex 2:	The General Status of the European Environment	157
A.2.1	Air quality	160
A.2.2	Water quality	161
A.2.3	Soil quality	163
A.2.4	Waste	164
A.2.5	Biological diversity	165
A.2.6	Public opinion in the EU towards the environment	165
A.2.7	Economic aspects of environmental pollution	166
A.2.8	Environmental expenditure	167
A.2.9	Summary	167
Annex 3:	Phase I respondents	171
Annex 4:	Phase II respondents	177
Annex 5:	Interview guide for companies	191
Annex 6:	Interview guide for institutions of higher education	197
Annex 7:	Material analysis structure No. 1 for companies	203
Annex 8:	Material analysis structure No. 2 for companies	207
Annex 9:	Material analysis structure for institutions of higher education	213
Annex 10:	Environmental courses offered by the analysed institutions of higher education: A structured tabular presentation of the information in paragraph 4.1.4	217

LIST OF FIGURES

Figure 2.1	Respondents distribution by country	34
Figure 2.2	Respondents distributed by industry	34
Figure 2.3	Details of environmental policy	40
Figure 2.4	Areas for details of environmental policy	41
Figure 2.5	Report on progress	44
Figure 2.6	Report on performance in various areas	45
Figure 2.7	Information on future plans	69
Figure 2.8	Areas of implementation for future plans of environmental policy	71
Figure 3.1	The Environmental Organisation	81
Figure 3.2	The basic structure of an input/output description	91
Figure 4.1	UK environmental managers' methods of developing expertise	113
Figure 6.1	Evolutionary stages of corporate environmental reporting	134
Figure A.1	Pb & SO_2 emissions and CFC consumption	160
Figure A.2	Water quality in the Rhine	162
Figure A.3	Municipal waste (1000 t)	164

LIST OF TABLES

Table 6.1 Evolutionary stages of corporate environmental management   132

Table 6.2 Evolutionary stages of higher environmental management education   143

Table A.1 Index of environmental impact in the EU Member States and various characteristics   169

LIST OF ACRONYMS

μ	Physical down scaling parameter (micro = 10^{-6})
Al	Aluminium
BAUM	Bundesdeutscher Arbeitskreis für Umweltbewußtes Management e.V. - a German organization similar to TREE (Joined Technology, Research, Enterprise, and the Environment) in the UK
BS7750	British Standard 7750 - an environmental management system developed by British Standard
CEDEFOP	Centre Européen pour le développement de la formation professionnelle (European Centre for the Development of Vocational Training)
CEO	Chief Executive Officer
CERM	Corporate Environmental and Resource Management
CFC	Chloro-Flouro-Carbons
CO	Carbon Monoxide
CO_2	Carbon Dioxide
COM	European Commission
COMETT	A EU programme supporting cooperation between universities and enterprises
CSD	Corporate Sustainable Development
D	Germany
DB	Database
DK	Denmark
DM	Deutsche Mark - the German currency
EA	Environmental Audit
ECU	European Currency Unit
EIA	Environmental Impact Assessment
EIS	Environmental Information System
EM	Environmental Management
EMAS	Environmental Management and Audit Scheme - EU's

	environmental management system
EOP	End-of-pipe
EU	European Union
F	France
FEPAP	Fifth Environmental Policy and Action Programme
GBP	British Pound - the British currency
GDP	Gross Domestic Product
GDR	The former German Democratic Republic
GNP	Gross National Product
HQ	Headquarters
HRM	Human Resource Management
ICC	International Chamber of Commerce
ILO	International Labour Organization - a UN organization
INSEAD	The European Institute for Business Administration
IT	Information Technology
IUCN	International Union for Conservation of Nature and Natural Resources
KPMG	An international auditing company
kWh	Kilowatt-hour - unit to measure the amount of electricity
LCA	Life Cycle Assessment
LE	Larger Enterprises
m^3	Cubic metre
MA	Master of Arts - a university degree
MBA	Master of Business Administration - a university degree
Mn	Manganese
MSc	Master of Science - a university degree
NO_x	Nitrogen-oxide compounds
OECD	Organization for Economic Cooperation and Development
Pb	Lead
PERI	Public Environmental Reporting Initiative
PhD	Doctor of Philosophy - a university degree

PMS	Positivistic model of science - a theory of science
PVC	Polyvinyl Chloride
R&D	Research and Development
Sb	Antimony
SD	Sustainable Development
SME	Small and Medium Sized Enterprises
SO_2	Sulphur dioxide
SO_x	Sulphur-oxide compounds
SPSS	Statistical Package for the Social Sciences - a computer programme
TEM	Training in Environmental Management - the project behind this report
TPLCA	Total Product Life Cycle Assessment
TQM	Total Quality Management
UETP	University Enterprise Training Partnerships
UK	United Kingdom
UN	United Nations
UNCED	United Nations Committee on Environment and Development
UNEP	United Nations Environmental Programme
US	United States of America
USD	US Dollar - the US currency
VOC	Volatile Organic Compound
VP	Vice President
WCED	World Commission on Environment and Development
WICE	World Industry Council for the Environment
WICEM	World Industry Conference for Environmental Management

TRAINING IN ENVIRONMENTAL MANAGEMENT: CORPORATE ENVIRONMENTAL AND RESOURCE MANAGEMENT AND EDUCATIONAL REQUIREMENTS

EXECUTIVE SUMMARY

1.0 INTRODUCTION

1.1 Background

One of the main themes of the Treaty on European Union (the Maastricht Treaty) is the promotion of environmentally sustainable development. The Union's environmental policy is based on the idea of preventive measures and the belief that environmental damage must be prevented at the source (section XVI, Article 130R). In the implementation of the Treaty, the Commission explicitly stressed that it would take full account of the environmental impact of industrial development and the principle of sustainable growth. The general principles of the EU's environmental policy are laid down in the Single European Act, and most recently incorporated in the Fifth Environmental Policy and Action Programme.

Specific attention has been given in EU environmental policy to the importance of the educational requirements which follow the implementation of cleaner and less harmful practices. The document "Industrial Competitiveness and Protection of the Environment" (COM 1992c) assigns a particularly important role to institutions of higher education, since their experiences in environment-related questions and development of new knowledge can be exploited by industry.

1.2 Research objectives

The aims of the TEM project are (for Denmark, France, Germany, and the UK) to:

- examine the development and trends in corporate strategies which incorporate environmental considerations;

- identify new managerial requirements following the preparation and implementation of sustainability-oriented business practices;

- analyse and assess new educational requirements following the implementation of sustainability-oriented business practices;

- provide a broad indication, through examples, of the range of approaches and measures undertaken by innovative companies and business schools which have adopted an environmental profile.

1.3 The study focuses on how some of the "best" industrial environmental and environmental management educators meet the environmental challenge.

1.4 It was primarily larger enterprises and Institutions of Higher Education in the northern Member States which proved to meet the requirements of the study best, since most of the activities and experiences in this field to date are found in this part of the Union.

1.5 A Definition of Corporate Environmental and Resource Management

In a previous study of the Foundation, environmental management was defined as: "the control and prevention of pollution to different environmental media (water, air, land) via "end-of-pipe" technologies; the adoption and use of "cleaner" technologies which generate fewer emissions, via product modification and materials substitutions; the recycling of waste products; and the management and disposal of pollutants" (Ecotec, 1992, p. xii).

Here, the term Corporate Environmental and Resource Management (Ulhøi, 1991), or, simply, Sustainable Corporate Management, is used, and is defined as: *a corporate strategy which does not erode the future biophysical possibilities for industrial and ecological development.* This relates more closely to a vital part of the "Brundtlandian" concept of sustainability, and emphasises the fact that there might be other important and related dimensions than simply environmental ones. In other words, the focus is on a corporate managerial approach based on the recognition of the inseparability between economic and ecological systems, the necessity of including internal as well as external environmental impacts, and the will to act as agents of changing values.

The concept of corporate sustainable development (CSD) introduced and implemented in this study confines itself to the following dimensions and goals: the growth/development controversy, values, technology, and ecological preservation and changing values. It thus leaves the structural and political goals to the politicians.

1.6 A Definition of Management and Training Needs

This study has also adopted the term "training needs" to reflect the fact that the "market", i.e. companies, might not be fully aware of all the requirements needed to improve their environmental "performance", and that equally, educators might not be fully aware of the needs of the market, i.e. among industrial companies wanting to "change course" to a more sustainable development.

1.7 Method of Approach

The study combines insights from existing research with original research to provide a state-of-the-art picture of the best practice in the Union as regards corporate environmental and resource management and the educational and training requirements of existing and future managers. The main elements of the overall approach included: an extensive literature review, interviews with key representatives of both national and international organisations who had been concerned with the topic for some time, a postal survey of existing researchers and other resource persons in the field, an analysis of several thousand pages of available corporate environmental material from more than 61 firms - of which approximately one third were visited and interviewed - and a similar amount of material from 40 higher education and research institutions - approximately half of which were visited and interviewed. The interviews were based on a semi-structured approach and included managers and professors involved in the subject.

Although some of the members of the research team had been very active in this area for quite a while, the decision was taken to seek outside advice on the choice of the "right" innovative and environmental examples in the four Member States concerned. A list of leading international researchers was therefore compiled in cooperation with both national and international colleagues (see, for example, annex 3) and these researchers were asked to provide examples of the leading and most innovative environment-oriented companies and business schools from both within and outside the four Member States (3-4 examples from industry, 2-3 examples from higher education, and 1-2 examples from other full-time educational courses). This resulted in a list of 150 companies and institutes of higher education, selected on the basis of their environmental initiatives (see, for instance, annex 4), which strongly indicates that the four selected countries (F, UK, D, & DK) are among the most progressive in the Community in this area. All available material from these organisations, including some examples from outside the four selected EU countries, was subject to extensive analysis.

2.0 CORPORATE ENVIRONMENTAL AND RESOURCE MANAGEMENT AND INITIATIVES: STATE OF THE ART

2.1 Corporate Environmental Practices

The study found that leaders in environmental management also tend to be large and innovative companies. In such companies, the basic steps for the greening process were typically taken more than one or two decades ago.

2.2 Characteristics of Existing Practices

For all 61 companies, the main characteristics of existing practices were analysed with respect to: (i) general information, (ii) values, objectives and strategies, (iii) operations, production and products, (iv) management systems and organisational structure, (v) accounting, auditing and allocation of resources, (vi) human resources, (vii) marketing and distribution, (viii) technology and R&D, and (viii) external relations. For the 20 companies which were visited and interviewed, the following dimensions were also included: (i) general information about the firm's environmental situation, (ii) drivers of the company's greening activities, (iii) the respondent's opinion on educational requirements, (iv) specific company approaches and initiatives, (v) communication strategies, and (vi) future expectations.

More specifically, the study found that:

- environmental managers in the environmentally leading companies had very different professional backgrounds (predominantly technical academics);

- the most frequently mentioned drivers were environmental legislation, customer demand, and corporate image;

- many of the interviewed companies aimed at going further than existing environmental regulations, thus indicating a strong need for becoming and/or remaining a pro-active company;

- the majority of companies visited had some kind of environmental management system, although several did not ever expect to adopt BS7750 or EMAS, as they feared that joining such programmes would result in a lot of bureaucracy and paperwork;

- a "classical" approach also found in this study was to let the environment manager coordinate and promote environmental policy;

- companies with a long history of involvement in security and the working environment had typically established a Safety, Health and Environment Department where environmental management issues were primarily handled;

- alternatively, an Environmental Council or Environmental Steering Group or Committee had been set up, consisting of key managers from various departments (and, in a couple of cases, of external environmental authorities), which reviewed progress and policy on environmental matters;

- in LEs, the strategic aspects of environmental management were typically the responsibility of the president, VP, or environment manager, whereas the operational managerial functions were often heavily decentralised;

- most of the corporate environmental information analysed in this study was qualitative in nature;

- many companies explicitly stressed that they intended developing quantitative environmental performance indicators in the near future (presumably in the form of eco-balances or LCAs);

- a considerable number of companies were found to use environmental audits or reviews. More often than not, such activities were mainly carried out for internal reasons. In several cases they were performed regularly;

- environmental management practices relied, to a large extent, on having sufficient internal capability to gather, process, and store environment-related data, as well as making sure that the "right" employees had easy access to such data. Such systems were found in several of the companies visited;

- no company used specific budgetary allocation and/or financial evaluating procedures for environmental activities and investments.

- companies often encouraged and tried to improve employee commitment, using a multitude of approaches, among which internal training was frequently mentioned as being important;

- most companies had several internal channels of information in order to ease and/or speed up the level of employee awareness. Most of the information was written material and distributed regularly;

- there were differences in the various teaching approaches adopted, ranging from "traditional" one-way teaching approaches, through very interactive and participative forms, to distance learning. In other cases, teaching-related corporate activities also included external stakeholders, such as suppliers, industrial customers, and schoolchildren;

- a frequently expressed requirement for environmental management was the need to be trained as a generalist;

- many respondents had a very clear message for management educators and institutions: environmental issues need to be fully integrated into all existing disciplines and courses;

- the larger the company, the more extensively involved it tended to be in environmental management issues;

- the majority of companies visited felt that they had a constructive and generally positive relationship with important external stakeholders, such as local environmental regulators and neighbours;

- a few companies expressed some optimism about the future, and thought that several of the existing trends of environmental legislation, environmental R&D, and the development of environmental management tools would continue in the near future; and

- a couple of firms expected a gradual corporate commitment to the other important pillars of sustainability (poverty, population growth, and the distribution of wealth).

3.0 EXAMPLES OF ENVIRONMENTAL MANAGEMENT PRACTICES

This section provides a summary of the range of corporate responses to the environmental challenge from leading industrial firms in the Union. It is important to realize that, although the impression gained from the interviews and the analysis of available material appears to be credible, the research team was not given the opportunity to substantiate the validity of the information obtained. This would have required very intensive investigations over a much longer period of time (i.e. several visits and unlimited access to all information and staff necessary). Budgetary constraints, however, prevented us from pursuing such a strategy.

The first example focuses on the organisation of environmental affairs and the structure of the environment department of a large multinational service company. The second example describes how one company defined and incorporated its environmental responsibilities in a single vision and how this influenced the environmental education and training of its employees. The third example illustrates the general approach to environmental management taken by a large multinational company. This covers policy, responsibility, environmental standards, environmental development drivers, and key areas of improvement. The fourth, and last, example deals with the communication of environmental performance to company stakeholders, and shows how one company has tackled this issue by developing an environmental communication strategy.

4.0 ENVIRONMENTAL MANAGERIAL EDUCATION AND TRAINING: STATE OF THE ART

4.1 Training in Environmental Management

In the majority of institutions visited and/or analysed, graduate courses in environmental management-related issues were typically disciplinary and specialised in nature. None of the "normal" institutions offering a Master's degree had fully integrated the environment into existing curricula. In a few cases, however, a more interdisciplinary strategy had been implemented.

4.2 Characteristics of Existing Management Education

For all 40 institutions, the key characteristics of existing management education were analysed with respect to: (i) general information, (ii) current environmental courses, (iii) educational approaches and existing teaching materials, (iv) existing research activities (topics, aims, people involved, publications, etc.). For the 17 managerial education and research institutions visited, the following issues were also included in the analysis: (i) general information, (ii) the role of management education institutions, (iii) what should educators prepare students to do, (iv) what should be taught, (v) what deserves special attention, (vi) the "ideal" curriculum, (vii) barriers to a further greening of curricula, and (viii) expectations for the future.

More specifically, the study found that:

- there were some positive signs of change and a growing emphasis on environmental education in business schools and other institutions of higher education, though still in a minority;

- the majority of institutions visited and/or analysed offered graduate courses in environmental management-related issues, typically disciplinary and specialised courses;

- none of the "normal" institutions offering a Master's degree had integrated the environment into existing curricula;

- the key educators in environmental management in the selected sample came from a variety of professional backgrounds, none of which could exactly be said to be "tailor-made" for the job;

- social sciences, technical sciences and natural sciences were represented, with a predominance in the former;
- the most frequently mentioned driver was that of one or two internal professors being dedicated to the environment;
- environmental concern was typically incorporated into existing programmes in an unstructured, non-integrated way;
- the institutions included in this study offered environmental courses both at undergraduate, graduate, and post-graduate level, typically as electives among other (degree-relevant) courses;
- environmental courses typically had a limited number of participants (≤ 25);
- environmental courses were often based on the interactive participation of the individual participant;
- environmental courses had close ties with local industry (students were often required to do their assignments in collaboration with local firms);
- environmental courses were characterised by a multitude of teaching methods, only using the "traditional" one-way-communication approach to a limited extent;
- environmental courses were of very recent date;
- institutions were generally mentioned to have a very important role as opinion-makers and in having political influence;
- the greening process had been delayed by various kinds of barriers, ranging from external barriers such as scientific communities and providers of research funds to internal barriers such as colleagues and (particularly in the older and larger institutions) institutional inertia;
- current research activities at these institutions were characterised by being specialised and by being carried out in isolated research environments (no, or very few international collaborators);
- current research activities tended to be both carried out and described in an ad hoc manner, presumably unconnected with local major research

plans and/or programmes;

- only one of the surveyed countries had any major planned and interdisciplinary programmes with researchers from other countries; and

- with regard to the future, there was general optimism among the respondents that the greening process would continue.

5.0 ENVIRONMENTAL EDUCATION AND TRAINING RESPONSES

This section provides a summary of the range of responses of the management education community to the environmental challenge, reflecting the influence of the greening process on some of the most receptive management education institutions. Here, too, budgetary constraints prevented us from attending lectures and gathering information from a variety of informants, e.g. students. The first example focuses on the characteristics of an interdisciplinary environmental course and the problems connected with organising and running the course. The second example illustrates the efforts of one large university to develop an environmental MBA course. The third, and final, example is from a course in environmental business economics, which includes both interdisciplinary courses and a trainee period in a company.

6.0 FUTURE ACTIONS AND ACTIVITIES

This executive summary has described the key findings of the TEM study. The study concludes with a range of initiatives to be considered for further investigation and action.

The Foundation has an important and continuing role to play in the development and improvement of environmental education and training at all levels, in cooperation with the Commission, EU agencies, national governments, various educational establishments, industrial associations and the social partners. In the light of this study, however, there are a number of areas of activity which need to be developed.

More data are needed on state-of-the-art training of lower management and skilled workers. This will require support for further studies in this area adopting a bottom-up approach, in collaboration with CEDEFOP, the Task Force on Human Resources, and OECD. Examples are:

- support for further studies examining the extent to which executive board members, conditions of employment, and corporate investors act as barriers to the scope and depth of strategic greening actions taken by CEOs;

- developing new ways and approaches for Commission-initiated/supported networks among corporations to encourage corporate-wide greening;

- assessing the potentialities and limitations of knowledge transfers from environmental management systems in LEs to SMEs, and from northern to southern Member States;

- analysing and assessing fundamental corporate core values, beliefs, assumptions and motives in a representative sample of leading companies;

- analyses of how investor pressure and/or resistance to environmentally responsible practices will affect the corporate greening process; and

- validation of the assertion that the corporate sustainable vision is based on the assumption that a similar transformation is possible in social institutions and settings.

1.0 INTRODUCTION AND BACKGROUND

1.1 INTRODUCTION TO THE CONCEPT OF SUSTAINABILITY

The "rebirth" of environmentalism as we know it today dates back to the early 1970s. Two "events" in particular from the early 1970s - the Club of Rome's report "Limits to Growth" in 1972 and the UN conference on the human environment in Stockholm in 1972 - can be seen as important milestones in the development of an international environmental policy. The idea of sustainable development, as presented in the IUCN publication "The World Conservation Strategy" in 1980, various publications by Tolba (1982) during the late 1970s and early 1980s, where the idea of "Development Without Destruction" was first introduced, "The Global Possible" (Repetto, 1985), and last but not least "Our Common Future" (WCED, 1987), highlighted the role of market forces in the development process and the role of poverty and overpopulation in natural resource depletion. This led to efforts to define sustainable development in a world of conflicting demands. In the industrialised world, demand is related to affluence and maintaining a materialistic way of life, while in the so-called "undeveloped" countries, the main concerns are overpopulation, poverty, and political instability. In both "worlds", however, there is a strong need to represent both the needs of future generations and to recognise the essential value of self-regulating systems within the biosphere. Despite the built-in conflicts, the failure to identify the values needed for a successful transition, and problems of practicability, the Brundtland Report is fairly clear on the following four interrelated issues: (i) it points to the need for an integration of environmental systems and resources into economic systems and processes to preserve and protect the natural environment; (ii) the report draws attention to inequalities in the current distribution of environmental and economic resources; (iii) it focuses on the importance of equity between both existing and future generations; and (iv) it emphasises the need for a longer time horizon in human planning and decision-making. An interesting hint is given in the following quotation, however, where the report stresses the need "to develop new methods of thinking, to elaborate new moral and value criteria..."(WCED, 1987, p. 39).

In other words, sustainable development is more than just the integration of environmental considerations into economic decisions and concern about equity and the needs of future generations. The above-mentioned publications pledged to recognise and build on common interests. All are based on the basic idea that natural systems (i.e. ecological systems) and man-made systems (i.e. economic systems) cannot be seen and handled in isolation, but must be addressed together. It was recognised that the solution to the present environmental problems does not necessarily imply zero growth and development, only less traditional growth, i.e. a different development. Thus, in contrast to the early "limits to growth" years, the important issues are seen as the uneven spatial distribution and exponential growth of population relative to carrying capacity and the insufficient and/or irrational uses of natural resources (Turner, 1988).

In view of the danger of the concept of sustainable development (SD) becoming yet another "catch-phrase" of contemporary environmentalism, a thorough analysis and discussion of the concept is highly desirable. The precise meaning - and not least the corporate operability - of the concept is still not on the horizon, however. As Serafy (1992) points out, it has proved difficult to define without ambiguity. The ambiguity is by no means confined to the Brundtland Report itself, which sees sustainability as implying compatibility with natural resource limitations and the waste assimilation and carrying capacity of Nature. There can be little doubt that the concept of sustainability is intrinsically linked to these other related concepts - the former describes nature's ability to absorb the physical (including man-made) forces it is exposed to, while the latter is a denominator of nature's overall capacity to "survive" over time without the collapse of ecological systems (Ulhøi, 1994). Alternatively, it has been defined as the maximum load the environment can permanently support within the limits of the ecosystem (Milbrath, 1989) without reducing its ability to support future generations (Catton, 1987). In essence, therefore, the concepts of carrying capacity and assimilative capacity provide the basic meaning of ecological sustainability.

However, merging the idea of economic and ecological sustainability - as suggested in the Brundtland Report - gives rise to conflicting interests. Most definitions of sustainable development are couched in general, qualitative terms, and include a wide range of elements such as economic growth, equitable distribution of wealth within and between generations (Repetto, 1985; WCED, 1987; Catton, 1987), supply of resources (Pearce, 1988), environmental quality (Braat & Steetskamp, 1994), "eco-eco" co-evolutionary development trajectory (Norgaard, 1988), etc. Several definitions more or less explicitly address the complexity of "eco-eco sustainability", and recognise that SD has natural as well as structural origins (Redclift, 1987; O'Riordan, 1988; Hueting, 1990; Goodland et al., 1992; Karshenas, 1992; ILO, 1992). The objectives most often included in published definitions are: survival (e.g. Daly, 1980), satisfaction of needs (WCED, 1987) and welfare (Goodland & Ledec, 1987; WCED, 1987; Constanza, 1989), policy of equality and justice (Repetto, 1985; O'Riordan, 1988; Schmidheiny, 1992), and shifts in values (Milbrath, 1989; Schmidheiny, 1992; O'Riordan, 1988; Goodland et al., 1992). In addition, the concept of sustainability is complicated by the introduction of a multitude of interests acting at various organisational levels.

Pearce (1988) defines SD in simple terms as: (i) development subject to a set of constraints which restrict resource "harvest" rates to the levels of managed or natural regeneration rates, and (ii) the use of the environment as a "waste sink", on the basis that waste disposal rates should not exceed assimilation rates (natural or managed) in the corresponding ecosystem. SD, it has been argued, cannot be realised without a shift in human activities, which can only be achieved by (i) dictating environment-conserving measures for production and consumption, and (ii) directly changing production and consumption patterns (Hueting, 1990).

1.1.1 The Road to Sustainable Development

Repetto (1985) sees SD as a goal that rejects policies and practices which support current living standards by depleting the productive base, including natural resources, leaving future generations with poorer prospects than our own. In other words, current decisions should not damage the prospects for maintaining or improving future living standards.

Turner (1988) identifies three conservation rules for realising a "sustainable" use of natural assets: (i) the maintenance of the regenerative capacity of renewable resources and avoidance of excessive pollution which could threaten biospherical waste assimilation capacities and life-support systems; (ii) the guidance of technological change, so that wherever possible, renewable resources are substituted for non-renewable resources, and (iii) the formulation of a "phasing" policy for the use of the latter resources. The Global Possible Conference (Repetto, 1985) stressed that several critical transitions are necessary in order to realise SD: (i) a demographic transition to a stable world population of low birth and death rates, (ii) an energy transition to high efficiency in production and use, and increasing reliance on renewable sources, (iii) a resource transition to reliance on nature's "income" without depletion of its "capital", (iv) an economic transition to sustainable development and a broader sharing of its benefits, and (v) a political transition to a global negotiation based on complementary interests between North and South, East and West. Pearce & Markandya (1989) argue that sustainable development will only be possible when the present ecological boundaries are removed. Mechanisms for doing so include the application of relevant technology, management of renewable resources to obtain higher natural yields, investment in assimilative capacity, recycling, and a switch away from such exhaustible resources as oil and coal. This links the notion of sustainability to resource and technology use, and socio-economic development and growth.

A distinction between sustainable use and sustainability has been suggested (O'Riordan, 1988) where the former is seen as an alternative growth and planning concept. Here, sustainability is regarded as a much broader phenomenon, embracing ethical norms for the survival of living matter, the rights of future generations, and the institutions responsible for ensuring that such rights are fully taken into account in policies and actions. Following this line of reasoning, sustainable development is a necessary, but not sufficient, condition for sustainability. The objectives of sustainability cannot be met without incorporating the principles of sustainable development.

Goodland et al. (1992) refers to the four elements of sustainability - poverty, population, technology and life-style - but leaves the problem of how to muster the political will for painful, but necessary, changes to others. The Brundtlandian concept of SD, they argue, has elicited two opposing reactions. One reverts to a definition of SD as "growth as usual", albeit at a slower rate, while the other defines SD as development without growth beyond the carrying capacity of the environment. In this sense, the WCED report seems to be torn between the two directions.

The approach taken by the International Labour Organization is based on the view that sustainability can be seen from various perspectives: (i) a time perspective, i.e. the present and the future; (ii) needs, i.e. meeting the basic needs of the world's poor, (iii) limitations of technology and social organisation, (iv) equity within and between countries, (v) integrated approaches to policies and actions, (vi) natural resource management, and (vii) anticipation and prevention as well as rehabilitation (ILO, 1992). Constanza (1989) describes sustainability as a relationship between dynamic human economic systems and larger dynamic, but normally slower-changing, ecological systems, in which (i) human life can continue indefinitely; (ii) human individuals can flourish; (iii) human cultures can develop; but where (iv) the effects of human activities remain within limits, so as not to destroy the diversity, complexity, and function of ecological life-support systems.

Others (Karshenas, 1992; Redclift, 1987) stress the need to define SD in terms of structural change in natural and man-made capital stock (including human capital and technological capabilities), which ensures at least a minimum socially desired rate of growth in the long run. This rate of growth could then be defined in different ways, depending on the level of development and the specific socio-historical characteristics of the country in question.

In addition to the biophysical and socio-economic dimensions of nature's carrying capacity, Hardin (1991) has suggested introducing the concept of a cultural carrying capacity, since the carrying capacity and the standard of living are irreversibly related. The higher the standard of living, the fewer the people who can enjoy it if the biophysical carrying capacity is not to be overloaded.

The ideal concept of sustainability also includes values and ethical dimensions, e.g. through references to intergenerational and intragenerational differences between humans and other biophysical species. This in turn calls for a re-evaluation of the existing ethnocentric and utilitarian frame of reference used to interpret and assess progress towards a more sustainable development. These are weighty issues, however, which will not be dealt with in more detail here.

In other words, sustainable development is seen as a process of change in which there are no clear prescriptions as to how we should act, either now or in the future. The individual actor should try to attain "sustainability" by critically examining his/her values, behaviour and relationships, and asking whether or not they are sustainable.

1.2 THE EU'S FIFTH ENVIRONMENTAL POLICY AND ACTION PROGRAMME (FEPAP)

One of the main themes of the Treaty on European Union is the promotion of an environmentally sustainable development. The Union's environmental policy is based on the idea of preventive measures and the belief that environmental damage must be prevented at the source (section XVI, Article 130R). The Commission has explicitly stressed that, in its implementation of the Treaty, it would take full account of both the environmental impact of industrial development and the principle of sustainable growth.

The EU document "Industrial Competitiveness and Protection of the Environment" (COM 1992c) explicitly stated that protection of the environment has increasingly become a political goal and a necessary condition for further industrial expansion. The general principles of the Community's environmental policy are laid down in the Single European Act, and most recently incorporated in the Fifth Environmental Policy and Action Programme (FEPAP) (COM 1992b). It is assumed that environmental concern can itself lead to an improvement in the conditions and demands which are decisive for competition. FEPAP is based on the view that environmental consideration facilitates an improvement in industrial competitiveness in several ways, either by so-called differentiation, cost savings, and "first-mover" advantages in big new markets for environmental protection technologies and so-called environmentally-friendly consumer goods or by improving the construction and control of the production system, especially after the introduction of cleaner technologies.

Increasingly, the EU sees the crux of the environment-business relationship, i.e. the interplay between industrial competitiveness and environmental protection, as lying in the introduction of cleaner processes and products, as opposed to reactive end-of-line measures. The EU's environmental policy has thus become a decisive factor in determining international competitiveness.

As underlined in FEPAP, sustainable development can only be realised if environmental considerations are incorporated into economic and political decisions. FEPAP's concept of sustainable development is defined as a policy and strategy for continued economic and social development which does not overload the environment and natural resources on which the quality of man's continued activities and further development depend. The Commission defines SD as a development which (i) maintains the overall quality of life; (ii) ensures continued access to natural resources; and (iii) prevents continued environmental degradation. It is recognised that, in the real world, the concept of SD is ultimately linked to society's or a region's future prospects for development and success, and, in cases of individual firms, their possibilities for profits and losses.

According to FEPAP, the practicable way of achieving sustainable development is by: optimal and efficient reuse and recycling; rationing production and consumption; and changing consumer and behavioural patterns. The topics included in the programme are seen as a result of past mismanagement, and the most important problems recognised to be man's present consumption and behavioural patterns.

The following areas of activities are included: sustainable management of natural resources; integrated pollution abatement and waste prevention; reduced consumption of non-renewable energy resources; improved management of mobility; integrated measures with regard to the improvement of environmental quality in urban envinments; improved health; and nuclear safety and radiation protection.

To sum up, environmental policy has a central role in the EU. It is an accepted principle that tough environmental requirements should no longer be seen as a necessary extra cost for industry but as a means of ensuring sustained economic growth (the term growth is explicitly used in the EU document). Furthermore, it is unambiguously emphasised that this must be regarded as a turning point for the EU, and that the balance between business and the environment is the greatest single challenge facing the EU in the 1990s and beyond.

Particular attention has been given in EU environmental policy to the importance of the educational requirements which follow from the implementation of cleaner and less harmful practices. As previously mentioned, institutions of higher education have an important role to play, since their experiences in environment-related questions and the development of new knowledge can be exploited by industry.

1.3 SUSTAINABILITY - A BUSINESS ISSUE

In an orthodox economic sense, income has to be sustainable. An individual cannot continue to live at the same material level if present enjoyment is obtained at the cost of running down capital. As capital is eroded, the ability to maintain the same level of consumption is undermined. This is why accountants persistently argue that, in profit and loss calculations, capital must be kept intact. Keeping capital intact does not imply that it has to be preserved in its original state, however, only that allowance is made out of current income to restore lost capital. Thus, economic rationale does not block the attainment of a more sustainable future - on the contrary it ought to favour it. The payoffs due to more efficient and intelligent resource and environmental management are large. The present costs of switching to better policies and programmes are small compared with future costs of the damage that will inevitably occur if a different development trajectory is not followed. Tougher environmental standards and goals may improve competitiveness in that they may result in modernisation and innovation.

Progress towards sustainable development makes good business sense because it can create competitive advantages and new opportunities (Porter, 1990; Peters, 1990). But it also requires far-reaching shifts in corporate attitudes and new ways of doing business (Schmidheiny, 1992). If growing environmental concern is to be treated more as an opportunity than a threat, then a whole new strategic approach becomes crucial. The implications are far-reaching, and include a redefinition of the corporate mission, a realignment of the corporate value system, and a change in behaviour throughout the entire organisation (Ulhøi, 1992).

A recent report (OECD, 1992) assesses the current world market for environmental equipment and services at about USD 200 billion. This figure is forecast to increase at an annual rate of 5-6% to USD 300 billion by the year 2000. By comparison, the present worldwide market for chemical products amounts to USD 500 billion. The report predicts that the environmental services industry will become one of the main growth industries in the near future, with market increases projected at 7.4% per year.

A small, but growing, minority of business managers in different industries are beginning to see environmentalism less as a threat and more as an opportunity. To make money while at the same time protecting the environment not only demands the greening and cleaning of existing industry (e.g. through the introduction of energy-efficient electrical appliances, heat pumps, more efficient harnessing of solar, wind, and wave energy), but will also require a good deal of entrepreneurial or "ecopreneurial" (Bennet, 1991) creativity to turn environmental constraint into new and viable business opportunities. Many products which are today manufactured on a relatively small scale have promising market potential in an environmentally more concerned world. Examples include: infrastructures for recycled materials; simple, high-quality, recyclable packaging; the substitution of clean technologies for toxic substances; thermally efficient building materials; and more efficient and reliable public transportation systems (Ulhøi, 1993). Recycling has already become a multimillion dollar business with high growth rates (Nulty, 1990). Orders for clean process technologies are booming, not to mention management systems for waste handling and processing.

Many countries have huge environmental problems. The US Environmental Protection Agency has identified some 27,000 hazardous waste sites, with an estimated clean-up cost of USD 25 million per site. This works out at a potential cost of USD 675 billion, judging from past activities and production (Rubenstein, 1990). A similar pattern can be identified in all the western economies (cf. annex 2). The former communist countries of eastern Europe provide major opportunities in pollution control and environmental services. It has been estimated that DM 200 billion is needed to reduce air and water pollution in former East Germany to western levels (Business International, 1990). In Poland, a World Bank estimate puts the cost of reducing air, water and soil pollution at USD 25 billion over the coming decade (ibid.). In Hungary, a government study found that 72% of the country is seriously polluted. The costs to the economy in terms of human health have been estimated at around 3.5% of national income (ibid.). And in Bulgaria, the Parliament has proposed that approximately USD 15 billion - or 3% of the country's national income - should be spent on waste water treatment before the end of the decade, which will still leave 40% of waste water untreated (ibid.).

If we accept that SD requires a proactive concern for the needs of people in the future, then, ultimately, it will also require a new shared vision and a collective ethic based on equality of opportunities, not only among people and nations, but also between present and future generations. Mankind faces the inescapable challenge of establishing a sustainable co-evolutionary societal development. Over the past two centuries, industrialisation has led to increased ecological instability, which has resulted in increasing global warming, ozone depletion, acid rain, desertification, declining biodiversity, and an accumulation of non-degradable wastes.

If our commonly held natural assets are to last, unsustainable development cannot be allowed to prevail. Up to now, however, command-and-control strategies have only had limited success - the environment is still deteriorating. It is high time for a greater emphasis on the role and responsibility of individual (and privately owned) corporations. These are not only the primary drivers of economic development, but are also mainly responsible for many of the existing environmental problems facing mankind today. Furthermore, they own most of the world's economic resources and know-how (Gladwin & Welles, 1976) needed to develop new, cleaner technologies and products. Put differently, industry cannot continue to content itself with accumulating economic assets from a short-term perspective, but must increasingly realign itself in the direction of protecting and improving the world's natural assets.

As has been shown, the Brundtlandian concept of sustainability includes a variety of dimensions (ranging from needs, values, interests, growth, overpopulation and poverty, through the revival of economic growth/development, international trade and legislation, to energy use and technological development) and goals (equality, redistribution, population stabilisation, ecological preservation, the revival of economic growth and an expansion of the resource base). Corporate Sustainable Management is defined in this study as: An alternative, holistic corporate philosophy based on the recognition that (i) the individual company is part of larger, mutually dependent systems, and (ii) alone and/or together with others, the individual actively and openly strives to keep the negative impacts on these relationships at the lowest possible level across different levels of biophysical, geopolitical and spatial structures. This implies that the self-interest perspective will have to be replaced by a mutual-interest perspective. Unless this happens, the wider dimensions of sustainable development risk being overlooked. The ideal concept of corporate sustainable development (CSD) discussed in this study confines itself to the following dimensions - growth/development, values, technology - and addresses only the following goals - ecological preservation, changing values - thus leaving the structural and political goals to the politicians. It cannot be stressed too strongly, however, that (i) to speak of corporate sustainable management and development will require going beyond integrating environmental considerations into business activities along trajectories where the role and fundamental values of business corporations are reinterpreted in the light of socio-biophysical interdependency, and (ii) corporate sustainable management must be perceived as a continuous process of change towards the ideal definition of corporate sustainability. Environmental and resource efficiency must therefore be seen as an intermediate stage of development towards corporate sustainability, which in the end, of course, will depend on the extent to which strategic actions can be taken by industry and other social partners.

The world's natural resources are presently under enormous pressure. Soil erosion, desertification, acid rain, the extinction of species, and the greenhouse effect have all contributed to the present deterioration of environmental systems (cf. annex 2). Economic production influences the environment in many ways, through the consumption of energy and natural, often non-renewable, resources, and the production of pollution, toxic wastes, etc. Protection of the diversity and richness of natural resources is an important goal of our concept of CSD. This will require the minimisation of the negative impacts of production systems on the environment by, for example, conserving and rationing non-renewable resources (fossil fuels, metals, minerals, rainforests, living species, marine systems, etc.). Consequently, industrial activities which consume such resources need to be managed in a way that will allow the regenerative capacity of these assets to function.

Thus, CSD does not imply zero growth. As suggested by Goodland (1992), however, it might be necessary to distinguish between growth-as-usual and development. Growth-as-usual leads to an increase in the accretion of materials, whereas development implies the realisation of potentials, to bring something to a fuller, greater, or better state. When something grows as usual, it usually gets quantitatively larger; when it develops, on the other hand, it gets qualitatively better, or at least different. Quantitative growth and qualitative improvement follow different laws. Our planet develops over time without growing. Our economy, a subsystem of the finite, non-growing

Earth, must eventually adapt to a similar pattern of development. Alternatively, we could say that physical inputs must cease growing, whereas the value of outputs may continue to increase, subject only to the prevailing level of technological development. Of course, if the physical input is limited, then, according to the Law of Conservation of mass and energy, so is the physical output. This is equivalent to saying that quantitative growth in throughput is not permitted, but qualitative improvement in services rendered can develop with new technology. Quantitative growth, as argued by Goodland (1992), is not the way to reach sustainability. Society cannot "grow" its way into sustainability - the best it can hope for, if it succeeds in changing the present trajectory, is the possibility of developing our way to sustainability. In this context, it is important to realise that there does not necessarily have to be any causal relationship between wealth and welfare, since the latter, apart from a certain amount of "quantitative" input, also requires some qualitative dimensions.

CSD will require a redefinition of corporate values and vision. The latter defines the nature of the relationship of the firm to its natural and man-made environments. Depending on how this relationship is understood and accepted, it will have a decisive impact on CSD. Milbrath (1989) argues that corporate sustainability is a core value which defines the essence, or basic theme, of a broad set of values. Using sustainability as a decision criteria thus encourages strategic managers to look beyond the boundaries of the organisation and into the wider community in which it operates. As pointed out by North (1992), today's environmental business management practice requires the integration of environmental concern into all managerial functions, with the aim of reaching a sustainable balance between the economic and ecological performance of the firm. Stead and Stead (1992) claim that strategic managers who want to make decisions based on sustainability need five instrumental values - wholeness, posterity, smallness, quality, and community.

Before it can perceive the environmental challenge in terms of new business opportunities, management needs to recognise that it will affect all departments. Purchasing departments will have to find new, sustainable sources of supply, demand materials produced in ways which have a diminishing impact on the environment, and find new ways of reducing packaging and using more recycled materials. R&D can contribute by providing comparative environmental impact data, by identifying processes which use resources more efficiently, by finding new uses for waste products, and by contributing to the creation of more durable products. Marketing departments can help by providing more information about consumer preferences for environmentally-friendly goods, by defining new opportunities in terms of customer demand, and by developing marketing, distribution and selling methods which reduce environmental impact. Production departments can devise new processes which consume less energy and materials. Finance and accounting departments can investigate the benefits of sustainability, e.g. easier access to capital, reduced running and maintenance costs, and develop new ways of expressing performance in addition to the normal performance criteria. Personnel departments can look at the scale and speed of the requirement for new learning at all levels, and how this can be done effectively and economically.

Although the management and use of technology has contributed greatly to the present environmental situation, engineering and technological applications can provide the solutions to many of its problems. Furthermore, since the technology to solve environmental problems will be developed almost exclusively by industry, management policies probably constitute the single most important force in bringing this about (Heaton et al., 1991). In a corporate context, SD will, as stressed by Goodland et al. (1992), require a concerted effort to remould consumer preferences and steer wants in the direction of environmentally benign activities, while simultaneously reducing throughput per unit of final product, including services.

1.3.1 Conclusion

In the terminology of the World Commission on Environment and Development, SD will never be a fixed state but a process of change, in which the exploitation of resources, the direction of investments, the orientation of technological development, and institutional change are in harmony with an enhanced quality of life. It simply implies that the overall level of diversity and productivity of components and relations in systems are maintained (Norgaard, 1988). It therefore follows that a corporate vision of sustainability is dynamic, and will accordingly be revised as the need arises.

1.4 CORPORATE GREENING AND MANAGEMENT EDUCATION

If the goals of CSD are to be achieved, quite a few business organisations will have to be completely reorganized. This will give a key role to institutions of higher education. Training, which is an essential ingredient of environmentally sound and sustainable development, is a valuable tool in developing skills and in keeping pace with new technologies and new environmental policies. In this context, it is important to consider whether environmental training should be targeted to special groups and to ensure that preventive approaches are given a high priority. At the Second World Industry Conference for Environmental Management (WICEM) in Rotterdam, in April 1991, the need for education received much attention. This conference led to an Advisory Committee on Environmental Education being set up, consisting of the heads of four academic institutions and four major international corporations. The findings of this committee were later presented in a paper at the UN Conference on Environment and Development in Rio de Janeiro in 1992 (ICC, 1992).

Past studies have indicated that environment-related subjects are difficult to incorporate into existing business education. The main factors which characterize the environmental issue, and which at the same time make it difficult to teach, are suggested by Roome (1992):

- Systems thinking and analysis: Environmental problems and their solutions are interconnected in ecological, physical, cultural, economic and political systems through time and space. Environmental education thus requires analysis and thought based on the interrelationships of systems both at the micro and macro level.

- Holism: Environmental issues should be understood in their broader contexts. This is not the same as comprehensiveness, which is more to do with fullness of detail. Holism is a matter of perspective and should be aimed for, although it is difficult to achieve in practice.

- Interdisciplinarity: Systems thinking and holism provide the meta-disciplinary background. Interdisciplinarity, on the other hand, recognises that, while environmental issues and problems are analysed and investigated by means of scientific methods, explanations, management and solutions take place through social structures and responses. A combined science/social science approach is therefore essential in environmental education.

- Positive and normative approaches: Environmental education is based on both a positive and normative approach. Positive, in the sense that it involves describing and predicting the status of social and physical environments. Normative, in the sense that it involves pointing out different ways of organising and structuring individual and collective behaviour and choices, thus seeking a new, improved paradigm for the human-environment relationship.

Environmental education and management thus embody environmental ethics and values, are systematic in approach, holistic in perspective, interdisciplinary in analysis, and search for better concepts and practice.

Education in sustainable development involves contributions from various sciences. Dividing scientific education into natural sciences, social sciences, and technical sciences, Vellinga (1993) suggests that the contributions of each are as follows:

The natural sciences (e.g. biology, ecology, physics, etc.):

- Analyse and monitor environmental processes and the state of the environment.

- Increase knowledge of how to minimise the environmental impact of company operations and products.

In short, to determine the carrying capacity of natural systems (the context of human activities) and how human actions and numbers are related to it.

The social sciences (economics, law, philosophy, sociology, etc.):

- Identify and implement organisational changes so as to include the environment in the planning and decision-making process.

- Design incentive structures to encourage environmental concern.

- Increase knowledge of societies' relationship to the environment and the implications thereof.

In short, to clarify and determine the values, changes, implementation principles, ethics, etc., (the software) relevant to and determined by the relationship between humans and the natural environment.

The technical sciences (engineering):

- Identify and develop more environmentally-friendly technological alternatives.

- Increase knowledge of the environmental implications of technological design and technological alternatives.

In short, how the technology and physical structures of humans (the hardware) can be developed so as to have less impact on the natural environment.

Whereas industry used to see the costs of meeting environmental legislation as a major constraint rather than an opportunity, it has slowly begun to recognise the advantages, since products which meet the toughest requirements can be traded freely without any environmental restrictions anywhere in the world. Industry has the financial resources, knowledge and power to realise tremendous improvements of the natural environment.

Within the traditional structure-conduct-performance paradigm, environmental consideration can particularly be implemented in differentiation strategies and niche strategies. To realise this potential, the role and responsibilities of the company need to be reconceptualized and redefined. Constructive dialogues and new partnerships are required. Some of the explicit goals and dimensions of the concept of sustainability must be directly linked to corporate activities and integrated into their logic and existing notion of effectiveness.

Basically, it must be accepted that society cannot produce and/or consume itself out of ecological problems. Despite existing limitations, "traditional" quantitative growth is inconsistent with the idea of sustainable development and the concept of CSD. Changing core values and structural factors, such as the redistribution of wealth, stabilisation of population growth, and the development of new and clean technologies and energies, takes time - and time is what can be saved by switching to an environmentally more sustainable development.

As far as training and higher education are concerned, implementing sustainable philosophy requires nothing less than a total paradigm shift away from isolated and piecemeal specialization (multidisciplinarity) towards an integrated, holistic approach (interdisciplinarity), which recognises that environmental issues have both technical, economical, ethical and social dimensions.

1.5 RESEARCH OBJECTIVES AND DEFINITION OF TERMS

The main aim of this study is to identify, analyse and assess whether there is and/or should be pressure for merging economic and environmental considerations in actual business practices and in management education at business schools and universities in the four selected Member States. Specifically:

- to examine the development and trends in corporate strategies in which environmental considerations have been integrated;

- to identify new managerial requirements following the preparation and implementation of sustainability-oriented business practices;

- to analyse and assess new educational requirements following the implementation of sustainability-oriented business practices;

- to provide a broad indication, by means of examples, of the range of approaches and measures taken by leading environment-oriented companies; and

- to provide a broad indication, through examples, of the present greening of leading business schools and universities (from the same four Member States).

1.5.1 General issues

The Fifth Environmental Policy and Action Programme is likely to have a major impact on industry in terms of increased self-regulation and extended responsibility, supported by well-geared economic incentive schemes. As industry adapts to an environmentally more sustainable development, this can be expected to have a significant impact on management and employee training. A key issue in assessing these impacts is:

- to analyse and evaluate both the Brundtlandian concept of sustainability and the corresponding concept adopted by the Fifth Environmental Policy and Action Programme from the perspective of the individual firm.

1.5.2 Specific Issues

Based on specific management practices and existing undergraduate and graduate management training courses in environmental management in the four Member States, the key issues are:

- to analyse and evaluate the adequacy or otherwise of managerial and educational approaches, including potential discrepancies between present education and training and corporate strategies;

- to identify and/or assess existing and/or potential financial and technical constraints;

- to analyse and identify future requirements for environmentally sustainable management practices;

- to discuss the feasibility of developing a harmonised approach to environmental education and training in European business schools, and the measures required for this.

1.6 METHOD OF APPROACH

1.6.1 Objectives of the data collection

The overall objective of the data collection was to identify leading educational institutions and companies with regard to environmental performance. This was done to establish the present state of the art and to compare the intentions of the educational institutions with the requirements of business organisations. The data collection project was designed with this in mind.

1.6.2 Structure of the data collection

The data collection method was designed only after an extensive survey of the sustainability literature. The need to identify state-of-the-art environmental education institutions and companies led to the data collection project being divided into two phases. Phase I focused on identifying and contacting an extensive panel of leading environmental management authorities who could indicate institutions and companies with a high degree of environmental awareness. Phase II focused on contacting - and gathering information from - the institutions and companies referred to by the resource persons and started with the collection of all available written corporate environmental material from the companies and educational institutions concerned regarding their environmental initiatives. This material was analysed and the most interesting examples selected for personal, in-depth, semi-structured interviews.

1.6.3 Sample selection

Phase I

The selection of resource persons for the expert panel in Phase I was based on existing personal research networks and contacts, a survey of recent conference proceedings and lists of participants, and other related books and papers. Additional names were obtained from directories of institutions, organisations and government agencies concerned with industry, education and the environment. This resulted in 78 names of academics, practitioners and organisational representatives in 9 European countries, who were then contacted by letter requesting assistance in identifying leading environment-oriented European companies and educational institutions. Of the total number of resource persons identified, almost half (35) responded with the names of companies and educational institutions which, in their view, had distinguished themselves in practising or teaching environmental management (cf. annex 3).

Phase II

The educational institutions and companies identified by the resource persons in Phase I led to a list of 55 (predominantly) higher educational institutions and other providers of environmental courses, plus 88 companies in 9 European countries. These 143 companies and educational institutions made up the selected sample for Phase II (cf. annex 4) but are not meant to constitute a representative sample from which generalisations about European industry and educational institutions can be made. The sole intention is to indicate the state of the art in industrial environmental management and business environmental education and related trends.

1.6.4 The data collection

Contacting the respondents

In order to obtain general information about the sample, all 143 institutions and companies were requested to send written material on their environmental activities to the Aarhus School of Business. A follow-up letter was sent if there had been no response after three weeks. Of the 143 institutions and companies, 101 (70.6%) replied, i.e. 40 educational institutions and 61 companies. After analysing the material obtained (see below), the 39 most frequently mentioned companies and educational institutions were contacted and asked to participate in the TEM-1 project, i.e. the interview round. In the case of companies, the most senior manager below board level was contacted (typically the environment manager), and in the case of educational institutions, the professor(s) coordinating or responsible for the environmental management course. Two companies withdrew during the final preparations, however, leaving 37 companies and educational institutions to participate in the interview round (cf. annex 4). All the companies and educational institutions chosen from the total sample were from the above-mentioned four member states: the United Kingdom, Denmark, France and Germany. Apart from the fact that many of the resource persons from Phase I were from these countries, it is also worth noting:

- that Germany, France, and the UK are often characterised as the industrial locomotives of Europe;

- that Germany, France and the UK have the highest GDP in the EU;

- that Denmark and Germany have a long history of environmental protection and legislation, with above-average expenditures on environmental issues (indication of the state of the art);

- that in many cases, the "greenest" companies and institutions and most committed researchers and practitioners cited in the academic/practical/journalistic literature are to be found in these countries;

- that together with Italy, the UK, France and Germany control 85% of the environmental technology market in the EU; and

- that the main purpose is to provide an indication of the state of the art in general, not the general status in EU Member States, or to draw general conclusions about the EU as a whole.

The data collection method

Considering the individual environmental situation of each company and educational institution, the data collection method had to be flexible enough to allow the researchers to follow up interesting leads and issues. Therefore, both quantitative and qualitative information was collected. This required methods which allowed a degree of flexibility but also were standardised to some extent. To achieve this, a combination of material content analysis and the personal semi-structured interview were chosen. By analysing the information content of the material on environmental initiatives, a more general picture could be formed from which to select the most interesting cases for the interview round. The analytical tools are described below. The interview round was limited to one interview per respondent. The semi-structured interview guides on which the interviews were based are described below.

Developing the data collection and analytical tools

The tools developed were, firstly, the registration forms for the material analysis, and secondly, the interview guides.

The material analysis framework had to take account of the difference between the information published by companies and that published by educational institutions. Companies publish information about their environmental performance and initiatives for use by investors, customers, government, employees, local communities and other stakeholders. Educational institutions, on the other hand, publish descriptions of environment-related educational initiatives primarily for students and lecturers. The main aim, therefore, was to evaluate the content and form of the information in the case of companies, and register the characteristics of teaching and research activities in the case of institutions.

The first tool for the analysis of company information focused on classifying environmental management initiatives by organisational functions.

The following functional areas were selected:

1. The company's environmental values, objectives and strategies;

2. Operational functions, production activities, and the resulting products;

3. Management systems used, including information systems, decision hierarchies, functional divisions, etc., and, in addition, the organisational structure;

4. Accounting for and allocating company resources, auditing procedures and processes, and financial management;

5. Human resource management, including hiring, dismissing, training and motivating employees;

6. Marketing-, purchasing-, and distribution-related functions;

7. Technology and R&D, including the development of the technological base of the company and related research activities;

8. External relations, including activities related to maintaining, initiating and developing relationships with company stakeholders;

9. Other functions not included elsewhere.

This choice of functions is based on a framework developed and tested in another context (Madsen et al., 1994; Rikhardsson et al., 1994).

In this part of the analysis, company material is treated as a whole, and company initiatives are registered according to functional area, together with a short description of the activity in question. The source of the information (e.g. annual report, internal newsletters, information folder, etc.) is given to facilitate future reference. The purpose, characteristics and results of the initiative/activity in question are briefly described, depending on the detail of disclosure.

The analysis results in a more holistic but qualitative description of the company's environmental management approach, the functional areas the organisation focuses on, and a short description of initiatives. The structure of the analysis is shown in schematic form in annex 7.

The second tool, or registration form, for the company material analysis concentrates on classifying and analysing the environmental information disclosed in company annual reports and/or specific environmental reports. The aim of this analysis is to obtain an indication of the environmental information most frequently disclosed in these types of report, which are the ones most often used by stakeholders in gathering information about the company's environmental situation. The analysis is intended both to classify the information according to category and to see which type of information is dominant, i.e. quantitative or qualitative information. To facilitate statistical comparison of the information, the registration form is similar to the standardised "questionnaire" used in connection with the annual reports and/or environmental reports concerned. This methodology is based on the KPMG survey of environmental reporting carried out in 1993 (KPMG

1993), but adapted to the purposes of the TEM-1 study. The analysis structure is shown in full in annex 8.

The following types of information were included in the standardised registration form:

1. Independent variables characterizing the companies, e.g. nationality and industrial sector.

2. General information about whether the company had provided a copy of its annual report (and if so, whether it contained any environmental information) or environmental report.

3. Information registered from the annual report included environmental costs, the type of environmental costs disclosed (contingent liabilities, capital expenditures, etc.), information subject to mandatory audit, and any environmental information included elsewhere in the report.

4. The further classification of environmental information included whether the company had a detailed environmental policy statement, and if so, what it covered (e.g. emissions, employees, local community, etc.), whether the company provided details of its future environmental plans, and if so, what they included (e.g. emissions, wastes, product design, etc.), disclosures of company environmental performance, the disclosure of both positive and negative aspects, and information about environmental audits, either carried out internally or by external consultants.

5. Information about education and training is treated separately; the type of education, and the level, content and results are registered.

The third material analysis registration form concerns the environmental teaching and research activities of the educational institutions. As regards teaching, the aim is to clarify the main characteristics of environmental educational initiatives at the institution in question. Teaching initiatives are described along a number of parameters, including the type of educational activities, educational approaches, and the materials used. This results in a register of environmental management courses, educational approaches and educational materials. As far as research is concerned, the aim is to register all information about any environmental management research being carried out, the topics covered, the aims of the research, the publications available and people involved, participation in networks, etc. This gives an overview of the institution's research activities, including its characteristics and status. This registration form is shown in annex 9.

The intention here was to design an analysis for educational institutions similar to the one used for companies in the KPMG survey. However, the differences in information format, incompleteness of the materials received, and the relatively limited information received made this impossible.

On account of the two different types of organisations being surveyed, i.e. companies and educational institutions, two separate semi-structured interview guides had to be developed for use in the personal interviews.

The main aim of the company interview was to identify the characteristics of a state-of-the-art approach to environmental problems. The interview thus both supplemented - and was supplemented by - the extensive material analysis. Accordingly, the interview guide was divided into seven subject areas, based partly on the structure used for the material analysis and partly on the TEM-1 project objectives. The seven subject areas, shown in full in annex 5, are:

1. General information about the company, e.g. number of employees, environmental costs compared with turnover, and R&D costs.

2. General information about the respondent, e.g. role, education, and the general drivers of the "greening" process in the company.

3. The company's current environmental situation, including main environmental concerns, management attitudes to sustainability, and company attitudes to environmental issues.

4. Environmental management education and training, with a focus on employee attitudes, educational requirements, educational approaches,

employee motivation, and opinions about the current environmental education initiatives of business schools.

5. The company's approach to environmental issues, including descriptions and discussions of the environmental management system, the company's environmental organisation, characteristics of the environment department, evaluation of new projects, and main environmental strategies.

6. Environmental communication and external relations, including such issues as internal and external communication and stakeholder relationships.

7. The last area concerns both general expectations of the future and the likely development of environmental management.

As with the material analysis, the interview guide for educational institutions was divided into environmental management teaching activities and research. The six issues covered are shown below. The interview guide is shown in full in annex 6.

1. General information about the educational institution, e.g. scope, ownership, and about the respondent, e.g. role and function. Also included were the starting point and drivers of the "greening" process.

2. Environmental management courses offered, including type, level, duration, scope, the educational approaches employed and their characteristics, effectiveness, and design.

3. Research in environmental management, with a focus on topics, aims, results and future research.

4. The role of the educational institution, including the role in the "greening" process of society, what students of environmental management should be taught, and how environmental management is best taught.

5. Barriers to and difficulties in implementing environmental management education, both expected and actual.

6. Future expectations and developments.

All interviews were conducted by two interviewers (a senior researcher together with an assistant), using a cassette tape recorder and field notes. One interviewer concentrated on asking the questions and guiding the interview while the other took notes. After the interview was over, the field notes were keyed into a computer while the interview was still was fresh in the minds of the interviewers. On their return from an interview tour, the tapes were listened to, and any vital information not caught the first time was subsequently keyed in, supplementing the information already entered and correcting misinterpretations. Compared with "standard" methods, in which interviews are typically carried out by students or other third parties and the transcripts typed by secretaries, this "dual" approach not only increases the validity and reliability of the data, but also optimises the time available. It should thus be noted that the registration method used in transcribing the tapes is not "ad verbatim" but transcription by issue, i.e. the respondent's answer and conclusion to a specific question is registered in shortened form, and not necessarily in the respondent's own words. However, the precise meaning and context of the responses are the same. All 37 cassette tapes (approximately 90 minutes each) are in the files.

1.6.5 Analysing the data

The material received consisted of annual reports, environmental reports, special reports, curricula, syllabuses, videos, press materials, articles on the environment, leaflets, booklets, books, folders, etc., amounting to several thousand pages in all. The material analysis resulted in 2 reports of approximately 100 pages each. The material analysis and interview transcriptions were then pooled into two reports, one for companies and one for educational institutions, in all 600 pages. Analysing the interview transcriptions and the material analysis results, and then structuring the information into issue groups, resulted in two approximately 40-page syntheses for each group. These two syntheses constitute the actual results of the survey, and are reported in a further condensed form in this report.

The results of the annual report and environmental report analysis were analysed using the SPSS statistical program.

In reading this report, the following should be kept in mind:

- all participants have been guaranteed full confidentiality - thus, no specific information can be linked to either an individual company or educational institution in the report;

- it is not the research team's intention to rank companies or educational institutions according to environmental performance.

2.0 CORPORATE ENVIRONMENTAL & RESOURCE MANAGEMENT: STATE OF THE ART

2.1 CORPORATE ENVIRONMENTAL PRACTICES

2.1.1 General information

This section includes the results of the analyses of environmental management practices in all the surveyed companies. The structure of the section generally follows the structure of the analyses.

A total of 84 companies were asked for information concerning their environmental efforts. 61 companies responded to the request either in the form of an annual report, an environmental report, or other material, i.e. a response rate of 73%. Of these companies, 20 were interviewed either personally or, in a couple of cases, by telephone.

It should be kept in mind that the material analysis is based on a limited number of observations, and that the respondents were not selected randomly, but by a selective sampling procedure.

2.1.2 Company Profiles

Companies from 9 countries were contacted, but material was only received from 6 countries. The number of companies responding to the request for information from each country is shown in figure 2.1. The 3 countries which failed to respond only represented a very few of the examples mentioned by the resource persons.

Figure 2.1. Respondents distributed by country

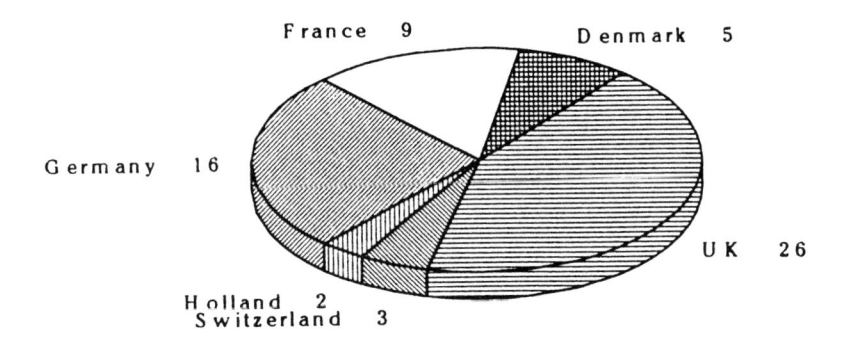

France 9
Denmark 5
Germany 16
UK 26
Holland 2
Switzerland 3

As can be seen from figure 2.1, most of the examples come from the UK, followed by Germany and France. This reflects response rates, size, and the selection procedure involved, of course, but also, to some extent, the greening process.

The companies have been classified into industrial sectors, as shown in figure 2.2. Chemical companies account for nearly 30% of the total, which is not surprising, since this sector was among the first to be controlled and monitored by public authorities due to its heavy impact on the environment. This also applies to companies producing metals or metal products, the electronics industry, and power production, etc. Surprisingly, however, the

Figure 2.2. Respondents distributed by industry

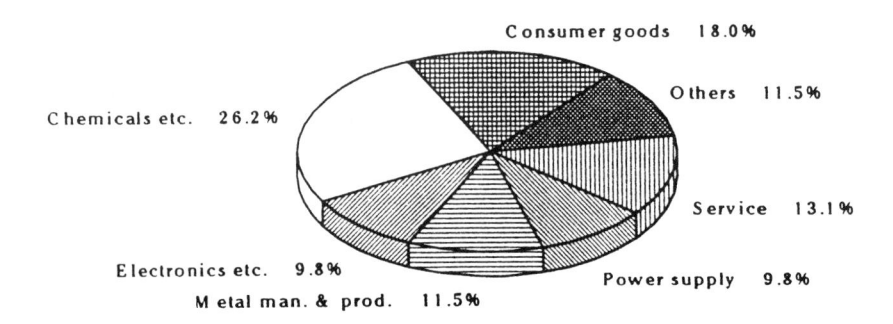

Consumer goods 18.0%
Others 11.5%
Chemicals etc. 26.2%
Service 13.1%
Electronics etc. 9.8%
Power supply 9.8%
Metal man. & prod. 11.5%

consumer goods sector is not that well represented. This sector includes companies involved in food production, textiles, retailing and cosmetics. The same applies to the service industry, which includes airline companies and telecommunications companies. The residual group "Others" includes companies in the paper, glass, and plastics industries.

20 of the companies sent a copy of their annual report, 16 of which mentioned environmental issues. The chemical industry is one of the industries in which environmental issues are normally mentioned in the annual report. However, the general impression was that exact information is very limited, and when included was mainly qualitative. All in all, only one company reported environmental costs in the financial statements, and only two reported them in the notes to the financial statements – one of which included qualitative as well as quantitative information. The three companies gave details on such items as environmental costs in their capital expenditures, site repair or restoration costs, and contingent liabilities, but there were no disclosures about environmental costs in future commitments, accounting policies or other items. Two of the companies reported on 2 items and the third on a single item only.

Five of the companies included qualitative comments on the environment in the managing director's report, and one included quantitative comments, whereas 10 companies included similar qualitative comments elsewhere in the annual report, and two included both qualitative and quantitative comments.

34 of the companies supplied a separate environmental report or similar material. Since issuing an environmental report is a sign of greater involvement in environmental matters, it is not surprising to find that the quality of the information is at a higher level, even though most of it is still qualitative. Special environmental reports are issued frequently in Germany and the UK, unlike in Denmark, where none of the responding companies returned a special environmental report. To be fair, however, it should be

noted that most of the Danish companies included environmental information in their annual report. In the chemical, electronics, and power generation & distribution industries, the frequency of a special environmental report is very high. In fact, more than 70% of the companies in these three industries sent a special environmental report, and the service industry was not far behind. However, it was surprising to see that none of the companies in the metal industry sent back a special environmental report, and only a single company in this industry included environmental information in its annual report. Of the 16 companies which included environmental information in their annual report, 9 also sent a special environmental report, and two who did not send a copy of their annual report sent a special environmental report instead.

The study includes both small and medium-sized enterprises as well as large corporations, though the latter dominate. The total turnover and total number of employees of the selected sample range from a low of a few million GBP to a high of more than 20 billion GBP, and from less than 150 employees to 375,000 (worldwide). There are companies with only a limited number of products and companies with up to 80,000 different products.

2.1.3 Information about the respondents

The general impression was that the typical environment department in the sample consisted of a small group of highly skilled and specialised engineers and/or chemists, most of whom had a PhD in their respective fields. None of the employees in the companies visited were originally trained in environmental management.

The professional background of the person or persons responsible for environmental management in the companies visited varied widely, ranging from engineering (e.g. process engineering, chemical engineering, mechanical engineering) and natural sciences (e.g. biochemistry, chemistry, physics, medicine, and biology) to social sciences (law). The environment department at one of these companies was truly multidisciplinary, consisting of a hydrogeologist, toxicologist, energy engineer, language expert, and a mathematician! Future employees were expected to come from economics, medicine and/or geography.

In another of the visited companies, there was close collaboration between the environment manager and the financial manager (who, incidentally, was originally trained as a nuclear engineer).

2.1.4 Drivers of environmental management

Drivers of corporate environmental management can roughly be classified as external or internal. The number of different external primary corporate drivers mentioned was almost as great as the number of companies in the study. They included:

- environmental legislation;

- customer demand;

- corporate image;

- competition;

- pressure from the general public; and

- media and/or pressure groups.

Legislation, customer demand, and corporate image were the most frequently mentioned external drivers, and quite a few of the respondents mentioned several of these factors.

Similarly, a very heterogeneous picture emerges of the internal drivers of corporate environmental management. Some of the internal drivers mentioned were:

- cost reduction (primarily viewed as an economic factor rather than a strictly environmental factor);

- previous safety experiences;

- the existing environment department;

- the existing public affairs department;

- employee satisfaction and image; and

- personal commitment of top management.

Again, no strong pattern emerges, though several did mention the existing environment department (which was typically headed by one very committed person) and employee satisfaction as the most important internal drivers. Contrary to expectation, however, only a few environment managers mentioned top management as the prime internal driver, although the majority emphasized the importance of support and back up from top management once the process had started.

In another case, a special organisational arrangement, consisting of departmental green teams of employees with a special interest in the environment, was established from the start in order to speed up and support the process.

2.1.5 Main environmental problems

To a large extent, the main environmental problems of the companies visited reflected differences in the lines of business they represented. It should be noted that environmental problems were rarely described in the companies' information materials, although they could be inferred from initiatives mentioned and measures taken.

The most important corporate environmental problems included:

- environmental impacts from emissions of SO_2, NO_x, CO_2, VOC, and dioxin, noise, wastes, pollution of drinking water, dust, pesticides, solvent emissions (both at company and customer premises), cumulative effects (e.g. the contribution to global climate change), and radioactive wastes/releases;

- packaging, plus the recycling and reuse of product packaging;

- transportation;

- the phasing-out of chlorine-bleached products and the phasing-out of CFC gases in products;

- site problems, including the clean-up of old contaminated sites;

- energy consumption;

- handling, storing and transportation of materials; and

- solvents.

Several of the companies interviewed expressed a sincere concern for the global aspects of environmental pollution, and were aware of the global impact of their business operations.

2.1.6 Values and objectives expressed in corporate and/or environmental policy

Of the companies which disclosed environmental information in either the annual report or a separate environmental report, 26 gave qualitative details of their environmental policy, 6 gave both qualitative and quantitative details, and the rest provided no details whatsoever. Thus the majority gave only qualitative details (see figure 2.3).

Figure 2.3. Details of environmental policy

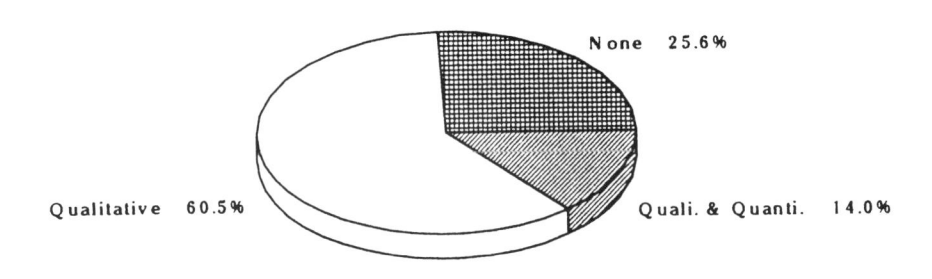

None 25.6%
Qualitative 60.5%
Quali. & Quanti. 14.0%

A number of companies gave more specific details of their environmental policy, though again mostly qualitative. The following areas were analysed:

- policy on air, land, and water pollution (19 companies provided qualitative information and 7 both qualitative and quantitative);

- policy on natural resource conservation (23 companies provided qualitative information and 5 both qualitative and quantitative);

- policy on legislative compliance (17 companies provided qualitative information, 1 quantitative, and 7 both);

- policy on employee involvement (17 companies provided qualitative information and 3 both qualitative and quantitative);

- policy on health and safety (14 companies provided qualitative information and 2 both qualitative and quantitative); and

- policy on local community issues (14 companies provided qualitative information and 2 both qualitative and quantitative).

Obviously, there is a slightly decreasing level in the content of the details (see figure 2.4).

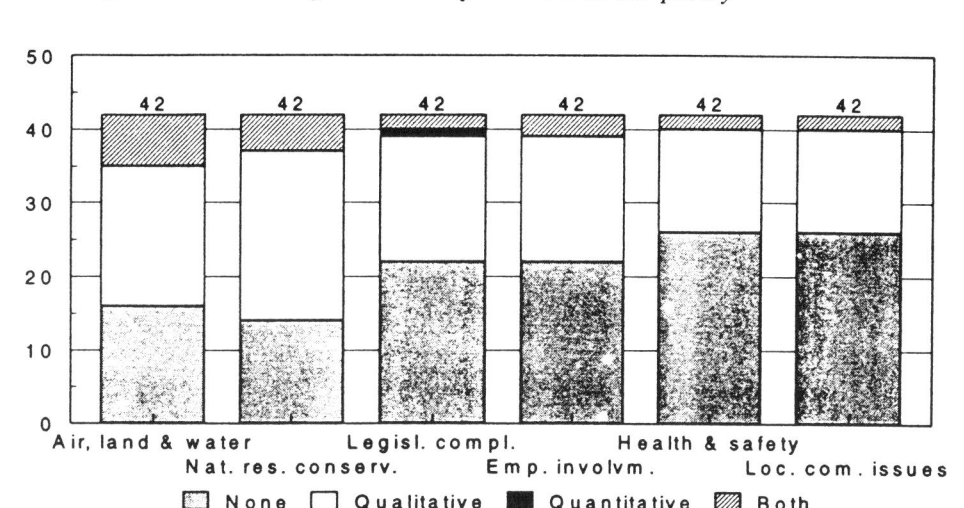

Figure 2.4. Areas for details of environmental policy

Only 4 companies gave details in all 6 areas, though as many as 10 gave details in 5 areas, i.e. approximately 50% of the companies which reported on these areas gave details in almost every area, though, as mentioned above, mainly qualitative information.

Oddly enough, it is mainly UK companies which include quantitative information - either solely or together with qualitative information. The surprise is based on the results of Peatie & Ringler (1994), which indicate that UK companies concentrate more on managerial and organisational change, in contrast to, for example, German companies, where technical and practical issues predominate. It is also surprising that companies in the chemical industry do not provide many details on their environmental policy compared with companies in the "consumer goods", "electronics & appliances", and "power generation & distribution" industries.

There is no straightforward pattern as regards the content of environmental policies. The most frequently mentioned environmental objectives were:

- being a good neighbour;

- meeting the most stringent environmental standards, and total compliance with the letter and spirit of environmental legislation; and

- surpassing the limits set by environmental directives and laws, and to come as close to 100% recycling and zero pollution as possible.

To some extent, there seems to be more agreement on the objectives of an environmental policy. Several described present national environmental laws as minimum requirements. In a couple of cases, the respondents were of the opinion that a corporate environmental policy must communicate the "right" environmental values throughout the entire organisation and integrate the environment into other business policies. In one company, environmental policy was part of a major company-wide Vision 2000.

A few companies have less formalised and/or decentralised environmental policies, giving individual departments more latitude to "green" their activities. One of the companies (a well-known UK manufacturer) had a very detailed corporate environmental policy, embracing a broad and detailed list of related environmental issues. This could, however, also partly serve an important PR function. Another interesting case probably had the most radical environmental policy of all. In this (also UK) company, it was explicitly stated that corporate environmental policy would always be given a higher priority than sales and profits, and that environmental protection would be given the same priority as commercial efficiency. This observation, however, strongly points to a longitudinal case study approach.

Again, it must be borne in mind that budgetary constraints allowed us no possibility to further check the degree of compliance with environmental policies.

The corporate environmental policies of the surveyed companies address a broad scope of environmental issues, including:

- water and air emissions;

- waste;

- packaging;

- energy and resource use, resource conservation, reuse, and recycling;

- external relations (e.g. to suppliers and neighbours) and communication (environmental disclosure);

- working conditions;

- LCA, cradle-to-grave product management;

- employee awareness;

- cleaner technologies;

- control and minimisation of accidents and risks;

- social responsibilities, including cooperation with local and national authorities;

- corporate citizenship, fair trade and ethics; and

- continuous training and education.

Many companies reported on their progress on these issues, though mainly qualitatively (see figure 2.5).

Figure 2.5. Report on progress

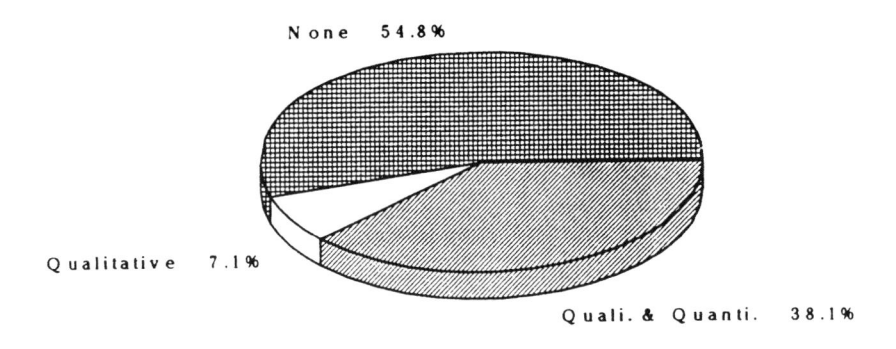

- None 54.8%
- Qualitative 7.1%
- Quali. & Quanti. 38.1%

It seems easier to report quantitatively when comparing with a previous situation. Again, UK companies take the lead in reporting on progress, and it is especially companies in the service and chemical industries which include such information.

In some areas, especially air emissions, effluents, waste disposal, and energy conservation, companies report performance very quantitatively. On the other hand, very few companies report performance in areas like accidents and incidents, and environmental costs and benefits (see figure 2.6).

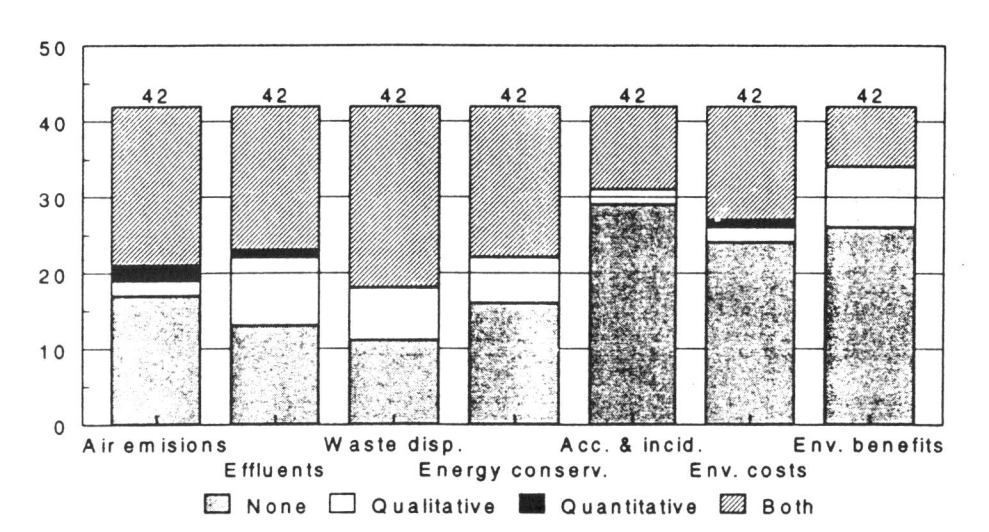

Figure 2.6. Report on performance in various areas

[Bar chart showing categories: Air emissions, Effluents, Waste disp., Energy conserv., Acc. & incid., Env. costs, Env. benefits; each bar totals 42, segmented into None, Qualitative, Quantitative, Both]

French companies are very good at reporting on their performance in almost all areas, followed by Germany and the UK, though at a lower level. It is mainly companies in the chemical sector and in power generation & distribution which give information on performance in general, though in areas such as waste disposal and energy conservation, most of the other industrial sectors are also well represented.

Some companies have chosen to adopt one of the existing environmental guidelines (e.g. the ICC Charter). Practically all the companies in the chemical industry have adopted the Responsible Care Programme.

2.1.7 Company environmental philosophy

It was a basic assumption of this study, supported by earlier experiences at the Department of Organization and Management at the Aarhus School of

Business, that the degree of corporate greening is strongly related to the extent to which a company can be characterised as proactive. Further experiences from the field of technology and innovation management have shown that, among other things, success can be equated with being proactive and responsive to change and new opportunities. The same applies to the environment. Companies which see environmental pressure and concern as a threat will never perceive the opportunities which this gives rise to, but only belatedly (often forced by legislation) react and adapt to the situation. Thus, a good corporate environmental performance indirectly reflects a high degree of innovative spirit, too.

Proactiveness is used as a differentiator during the analysis. In this study, however, the corporate respondents have been given the opportunity to present their own interpretations. Because of budgetary constraints, the researchers have been unable to test the validity of these interpretations.

The analysis of the replies of the companies surveyed shows that the majority of companies perceive themselves as proactive, though some stressed that there are areas where the company has to be reactive. Some also made a distinction between internal and external dimensions, e.g. one company said that they were reactive as regards customers, but very proactive as regards R&D - particularly when it concerns environmental legislation.

2.1.8 Environmental management systems and certification

It could be expected that environmentally leading companies are already, or at least soon will be, certified in accordance with, for example, BS 7750, since many of them already have quality certifications. Furthermore, several companies explicitly stated that quality and the environment went hand in hand.

However, only a minority of the companies analysed here were considering environmental certification. Several expressed deep concern about the

European Eco-Management and Auditing Scheme (EMAS), because they were afraid that it would become too bureaucratic and demand too much paperwork. On the other hand, several companies either had participated or were participating in pilot studies concerning BS 7750. Moreover, a couple of companies had participated in a number of pilot studies for BS 7750 and/or EMAS - despite the fact that they were among the world leaders in corporate environmental performance. These companies were quite certain that they could manage very well on their own. One company, a well-known world leader in environmental performance, indicated that if environmental certification became a European standard, then it would also become the standard for them.

Several companies said that they had adopted the same corporate environmental policy worldwide. One bluntly stated that, for global companies like itself, a European standard was not enough (though it could also be too efficient, considering the fact that the company in question has some of the fastest growing and most important market shares in countries with less stringent environmental regulations!). Another well-known company explained why it operated according to individual country standards but had guidelines for minimum standards: having fixed standards would hinder improvement. This respondent further pointed to the necessity of considering cultural differences. For example, environmental standards adopted in Scandinavia might prove unsuitable in Latin America, because local managers have trouble understanding why they have to follow environmental guidelines that are stricter than local legislation.

The lack of environmental certification does not mean that companies do not have an environmental management system in place, however. On the contrary, the majority of the companies in this study have their own well-developed environmental management systems. Some environment managers explicitly stated that, if they wanted to, they could be certified according to actual standards almost without changing anything in their present environmental management systems.

Others stressed that they had absolutely nothing against authorities helping industry with environmental principles and standards - as long as they only define what to do, not how to do it.

As previous studies have shown, eco-balances have been particularly popular in German industry. This was also borne out by this study. One of the German companies interviewed went as far as to say that their huge internal computerised database was the very nerve centre of their environmental management system. Apart from environmental data related to specific substances, such databases typically include information on, for example:

- suppliers;

- safety data sheets;

- operating instructions;

- environment-related technical data for plants;

- safety information;

- safety and environmental data for use in capital environmental investment;

- monitoring of plants; warehouse inspections;

- environmental assessment in the case of acquisitions;

- accident statistics; and

- training.

On the other hand, this very detailed approach at the operative and tactical level has, to some extent, been at the expense of a detailed environmental policy.

2.1.9 The organisational approach to environmental issues

The study found a variety of approaches in the way individual companies have adapted and adjusted their organisational structure during the process of environmental change. The "classical" approach, also found in this study, is to let the environment manager coordinate and promote environmental policy. Actual implementation is a joint effort between the corporate environment manager and division and plant managers. Environmental responsibility thus rests with division and plant managers, not with the corporate environment manager.

Companies with a long history in safety and the working environment have typically established a Safety, Health and Environment Department, where environmental management issues are primarily handled. Such departments often act as a corporate advisory group for the support and promotion of a number of different issues.

The larger companies in the study, with a number of rather autonomous departments, often pointed to the need for more "cross-collaboration".

Some companies had formed an Environmental Council, or Environmental Steering Group or Committee, consisting of key managers from various departments (and, in a couple of cases, of external environmental authorities), to review progress and policy on environmental matters. In addition to this, various kinds of working groups may be set up to take care of specific problems, and/or cross-functional management working teams established to create a forum for discussion. Internal environmental networks have also been set up in some of the companies to promote and help "environmental champions".

Another approach was to form cross-departmental green teams, which drive the environmental initiatives in each department. Quarterly meetings were held between the heads of the green teams, with the environmental manager playing a coordinating and information providing role. The implementation of environmental policy was also monitored by a senior executive.

Smaller companies with a less formalised structure have taken another course. Here, the environmental organisation is based around the production manager. He reports annually on production-related environmental issues and describes the plans, i.e. investment plans, for the following year.

In LEs, where the operational management functions are often heavily decentralised, the strategic aspects of environmental management are usually the responsibility of the president, VP, or environment manager. In one LE, the CEO himself was the sole person responsible for environmental policy and strategy, with implementation being delegated to the line managers. In several cases, such an approach has resulted in each division having its own environmental department. From a general point of view, this study has demonstrated that environmental strategy and policy issues are typically very much centralised in very few hands at HQ, with direct reference to the corporate VP. Yet another approach reported in the study has been to appoint environment managers at both plant level, regional level, national level and corporate level (VP). The study has also identified a compromise approach, which can be characterised as a decentralised-centralised approach. Here, each plant has corporate Environmental Commissioners who are directly responsible to the company president. Environmental Task Forces are established under each commissioner, who coordinates all environmental initiatives.

In companies where the environment and quality policy go hand in hand, the environment has been organised under the quality manager. In several of the companies, management has explicitly given operational environmental responsibility to the line managers.

In some companies, responsibility for environmental issues has been organised in an Environmental Forum led by an Environmental Advisor, who is also the environmental research manager. This forum includes both external and internal people. In one (high-tech) company, all environmental initiatives are coordinated by an interdisciplinary project team.

In other cases, heading the environment department has been placed as a staff function. In a couple of cases, environmental responsibility rests with the senior Technical Officer.

The general impression is that environment managers have some influence on corporate strategy and development. In one company, the respondent said that the environment department had the formal power to stop any strategic decision that had not taken the environment into account.

One leading manufacturing company employs waste coordinators, energy coordinators, EIA coordinators, chemical coordinators, and emission control coordinators.

Some respondents drew attention to the fact that there was always tension between departments when resources were scarce. One company cited the conflict which arose between, for example, the environment department and the finance department over environment-related investment when environmental and financial criteria did not match. The final decision lay with the Industrial Resource Department, based on information from the two other departments.

Middle managers were also mentioned to be a problem, because they had little time to devote to environmental problems and because they were caught between the shop floor and senior management.

2.1.10 Operational goals and initiatives

Various quantitative goals are published, including:

- CO_2 emissions (kg) per specified unit of product;

- total emissions of NO_x, SO_x; CO_2; and

- total annual fuel consumption.

Several respondents also stated that, wherever possible, their organisations sought to implement quantitative measures (see figures 2.3-2.6). According to one environment manager, quantitative measurements were necessary in order to set goals. Others felt that environmental management still lacked such measurement methods, however, and that, at present, energy use and waste were the only measurable variables.

In one case, the company had developed quantitative performance indicators unifying all environmental impacts into a single index for every impact area (air, water, waste).

One of the most "radical" environmental reports found in the study included quantified objectives for almost all the company's business areas. In one of the more extensive eco-balances (input/output), the monitoring and reporting system is divided into three balances: a company balance, process balance, and product balance. All measurements are in natural units. Following this approach, another company has implemented a reporting system based on material flows (input/output). Environmental effects are evaluated on a three-point scale. The system is used as an early warning system and in decision support.

Quantitative goals are typical of the German eco-balance approach, specified in natural units for each "account" of the eco-balance system. A company mentioned that, while it was not yet possible to quantify specific objectives for the group as a whole, 80%-90% of its divisions would publish quantitative goals by 1994/95.

2.1.11 Environmental management tools and methods

In this study, the term Total Product Life Cycle Assessment (TPLCA) is used to distinguish between the "old, or traditional" LCA concept, which dates back to the 1970s, and the "new" one, which is based on a cradle-to-grave approach (Ulhøi, 1994). While this tool is in use in many of the companies visited, the study allowed no possibility for examining how extensive TPLCAs are.

Many companies try to use TPLCAs wherever possible, but they are still primarily based on qualitative points of reference. Due to the enormous diversity of products, one respondent (a scientist) did not believe that really scientific LCAs would ever be realistic. Notwithstanding, TPLCAs seem to have become one of the most important tools in environmental management. Many see it as a vital decision-support tool, though at the same time recognise that it can never be 100% foolproof. As one respondent said, they were presently carrying out TPLCAs for some products to ensure that investments were based on the reduction of pollution at source rather than EOP measures. In this company's view, TPLCAs are the most important decision criteria.

In one of the companies visited, a risk assessment is automatically carried out if the Environmental Audit shows that there are no alternative solutions to the problem. In another company, TPLCA was used in all phases, from R&D to transport and post-consumption, as a priority-setting tool.

Again, it should be noted that budgetary constraints ruled out any qualified assessment of the quality and specific content of any corporate environmental management initiative.

Here, environmental review and EA are used synonymously (since there appears to be some confusion among practitioners), and is defined as strategic activities with the purpose of evaluating corporate environmental performance. No distinction has been made as to whether it is for internal and/or external purposes, or whether it has been carried out by independent external specialists.

In contrast to TPLCAs, which can be applied to products as well as processes and technologies, and which are predominantly prospective, Environmental Audits (EAs) are more "macro-oriented" in scope and, to a large extent, retrospective, since they typically aim at evaluating a company's recent and total environmental performance. There were descriptions of environmental audits in a number of companies' information material. EAs were mainly carried out internally. Internal environmental audits were most frequently reported by companies in the UK and France. There were no indications of any major differences between industrial sectors on this.

During the interviews, EAs were said to be of vital importance for top management in assigning priorities. In one company, the findings were classified into essential, very important, important, and desirable.

Several of the analysed companies have a continuous programme of environmental reviews (in some cases, partly assisted by external consultants). In the more "advanced" companies, this led to (at least) the following:

- an internal management report (limited circulation), with a lot of details for operational managers;

- a summary action list identifying which areas needed to be worked on by whom and when; and

- a summary report, distributed internally and/or externally.

The quality of such reports and other public environmental disclosures varies somewhat, and in only one or two cases were there examples of environmental disclosures which came close to the rationale of environmental audits as described in various guidelines and textbooks, such as ICC (1991). For a more detailed analysis of this, see section 2.1.17.

The majority of published environmental reports were dominated by good intentions and qualitative goals and disclosures. Published environmental reports included such areas as:

- systems and controls;

- procedures and responsibilities;

- noise;

- emissions;

- fuel efficiency;

- energy;

- waste water and other materials;

- conservation;

- environmental management and communication;

- VOC emissions;

- accident statistics; and

- environmental investments and plans, etc.

For further details, see figures 2.4 and 2.6.

In one of the visited companies, priorities were given according to a points system, which focused on the total effect of discharges (E), dispersion of discharges (D), and quantity of measure (Q): (QxExD).

The frequency of such corporate activities varies from once a year or every other year to every 3-4 years (to some extent depending on the size of the company), with all plants being inspected by EA experts from company headquarters. The general impression is that regularity prevails over ad hoc approaches or irregularity. The plants use their own internal rules and standards, typically adapted from those of the mother company. The yearly environmental objectives are regularly compared against the results during the year. All plant managers have to report to HQ.

At another company, different types of EA were used: compliance, utilities, waste, materials, air emissions, risks, liabilities (50 site audits were carried out here during 1993). See figure 2.5. for a general overview of the situation.

In a third company the EA was described as a pyramid of audits, based on self audits, compliance audits, internal expert audits, project reviews, process & system audits, and government/third party audits. In the latter case, the different audits were carried out with different frequency. Yet another company has chosen to conduct regular EAs in their corporate department, corporate offices and centralised services, whereas their plants are reviewed at random on a case-by-case basis in collaboration with the plant environment manager.

Information is often collected in one of two ways. Either the line managers automatically collect and prepare the information in accordance with internal procedures or the auditing team sends out questionnaires prior to visiting the individual plants. The impression was that the results were not intended to be used for punishment, but shown to and discussed with line management before being "officially" finalised.

One of the most "advanced" approaches found in the study was that of a company which had implemented an environmental accounting and reporting system containing input-output descriptions of the production processes, i.e. eco-balances. All substances were registered in their basic form, and the eco-balance was audited by an independent external auditor. In another fairly environmentally advanced company, each business unit had to audit its environmental performance as regards (i) compliance, (ii) progress vis-à-vis improvement plans, (iii) complaints, and (iv) operational learning experience. All sites were expected to maintain an up-to-date assessment report of their environmental impacts. In this company, the auditing activities included financial as well as environmental issues.

After completion of the environmental audits and/or reviews, the audited site typically received a recommendation list of areas in need of improvement. In most cases, the site had to improve performance either because of legal pressure or because it was faced with punitive measures from corporate management.

Companies in the process of implementing a fully developed environmental management system (BS7750 or EMAS) naturally follow the guidelines defined by these systems.

For all companies engaged in environmental management data collection, processing, storing, and having easy access to data is of vital importance. The German eco-balance approach, for example, is explicitly based on the existence of a well-developed corporate environmental database.

In one company, such an information system was based on an internal reporting system, by which data on the emissions of every plant were collected and aggregated once a year, giving an overall picture of corporate worldwide emissions. Another company had an Environmental Incident Reporting System which registered all incidents, whether they were reportable to the government or not.

"Basic" systems typically collect monthly data on fuel consumption, emissions, waste, etc. More advanced versions collect all the environmental characteristics of materials and substances purchased. One of the companies visited which used the Eco-balance approach explicitly stated that their centralised databases (DBs) constituted one of the company's most important competitive advantages. In this company, environmental monitoring and the monitoring of scientific literature were linked through the DB and acted as a decision-support system.

2.1.12 Financial and accounting issues

None of the companies had special allocation requirements and/or procedures for environmental projects. Projects involving legislative compliance tended to get a high priority in some of the companies visited. Cost-neutral, and especially cost-saving projects were also undertaken. The problems occured when the costs outweighed the benefits. Most companies said that they did not check environmental investments for financial performance.

It was also pointed out during the interviews that it was difficult to separate environmental costs from other costs - and probably not worth it. In a couple of cases, however, it was estimated that environmental investments represented 18-20% of the total investments of the companies in question.

Some companies accepted a longer pay-back period for environmental investments - in extreme cases up to 10 years - while in a few, the pay-back period was the same for environmental investments as for other investments. The rest did not seem to have paid any particular attention to this issue.

2.1.13 HRM and the environment

A couple of respondents argued that the best way of motivating senior management was through money and costs, and then through legislation and personnel liability. These tools should be used in the right "combination", however. At lower levels it was necessary to motivate people by explaining that "we need your help".

It was generally recognised that all employees had an important role in the success of corporate environmental greening activities. A variety of approaches were used to motivate the individual employee to support corporate environmental policy and/or do more themselves, and to foster new ideas. These included:

- monetary rewards (e.g. bonuses) or other rewards (e.g. internal funding);

- management demonstrating that "we need your help" (in word as well as deed);

- improved internal communication;

- increased internal training;

- increased dialogue;

- more cross-functional and cross-departmental meetings;

- clear goals and objectives, and visible and documentable progress; and

- including individual environmental performance issues in existing employee evaluation schemes.

Some companies put little faith in monetary rewards, however, and believed that employee motivation was best achieved by other means. Several assured us that their employees had a very positive attitude towards environmental initiatives and change.

In most of the companies visited, environment-related information was updated internally, mainly by means of:

- internal newsletters or magazines (quarterly, in some companies almost monthly);

- internal ad hoc leaflets, notice boards, reports, or special bulletins and articles in periodicals;

- continuously updated handbooks;

- ad hoc videos; and

- (centralised) briefing groups.

In a few cases, environmental news and information was distributed via an internal electronic information system.

In the main, corporate newsletters contain short presentations and descriptions of environment-related news (of relevance to the company). Bulletins or reports are used for more in-depth and/or specialised information and discussion.

Some of the interviewed companies had carried out (or were planning to carry out in the near future) internal employee attitude surveys. One respondent (from one of the LEs in the study) pointed out that one of the main reasons for these surveys was the danger of making HQ decisions without assessing employee attitudes first. A failed environmental training programme was mentioned as an example.

A recent survey in one company identified three key issues: (i) energy consumption per m^2, (ii) local community environmental initiatives, and (iii) training in environmental issues.

A couple of companies which had carried out such surveys mentioned that another purpose was to identify existing and/or future training needs. The survey was described by one of these companies as follows: A complete survey of environmental training requirements was carried out which identified a number of areas for improvement and the development of an environmental warning policy. Another survey of employee attitudes to environmental issues identified areas for improvement in (mainly) communication and training.

In a couple of companies, corporate management had carried out such activities prior to the publication of their corporate environmental report, among other things to test the communicative quality of the result before making it available to the public.

A large number of the companies in this study have developed various kinds of internal environmental initiatives, both for existing staff and/or new employees, ranging from "awareness-raising" courses to "maintenance courses". However, only 15 companies mentioned environment-related training activities in their information material. Very few went into detail regarding this training, and there was no information at all about the results of the training activities.

Some companies started environmental training several years ago. For example, one chemical company launched an environmental training programme in 1982. According to the respondent, however, this was not a success, owing to a lack of awareness among the employees.

The majority of training courses are internal. Some companies have cooperated with business schools in this area, however. The various training approaches cover:

- lectures;

- seminars;

- workshops;

- videos; and

- distance learning.

The main internal training approaches focused on corporate employees from middle management downwards. One respondent said that top management were not included because they were already heavily involved in these matters. Others gave no indication whether top management were included in such courses or not, however. A few companies (well-known for their environmental performance) did include top management.

Yet other companies integrated health and safety issues into their courses. The specific content of such courses varied according to their length, but ranged from just raising awareness (for new employees) to being specialised, internal courses for existing employees. In a couple of cases, the intention was also to include the company's customers. One manufacturer of surface protective materials has developed a training programme for their customers to educate them about the environmental effects of using their products and how to minimise these effects. According to the respondent, one of the main ideas behind this was to make the customer and user of their products think of product waste not as waste but as unused products.

2.1.14 Environmental management educational requirements

A commonly shared belief among interviewed environmental managers was that there was an indisputable need for generalists; in other words, a need for people with a fairly broad background and training to coordinate the necessary activities and to create and exploit the potential synergy. It was also generally accepted that there was still a need for a limited number of environmental specialists, however. Several of the managers mentioned that generalists also needed a broad technical background in engineering, science and technology.

A representative of one small company claimed that technical education was more important for a small company than a large one, which could typically afford a broader range of specialised employees.

One environment manager made the point that there was, actually, less difference in environmental attitudes between managers with different educational backgrounds than between managers of different ages or personal characteristics.

The respondents were unanimous in their belief that environmental issues needed to be integrated into business education. Several respondents suggested that the ideal (in the future) would be to incorporate environmental issues into all business courses at all levels. More specific examples of what environment managers feel to be important in management (i.e. non-technical) education today include:

- the connections and relationships between business decisions and activities and the (natural) environment;

- environmental economics;

- environmental regulation and laws; and

- environmental management tools.

Few were able to suggest how this could best be done (apart from idealistically integrating it wholeheartedly in all business disciplines). The case study approach and economy-ecology conflict issue were mentioned, however.

2.1.15   Marketing, advertising, and competition

Several of the companies in the study hold various courses for and/or to ensure that their suppliers are environmentally literate. Some companies had designed environmental training courses for some of their major suppliers. Such courses address a variety of environment-related issues, ranging from corporate environmental policy and the goals and requirements of the buyer to how to improve cooperation on environmental issues between buyer and supplier. Some of the more "radical" means used by the surveyed companies included an audit of all (or all major) suppliers and a demand for the documentation and verification of the supplier's environmental performance. This can lead to conflict, however. One of the companies interviewed told us that some of their suppliers viewed the provision of environmental information as a competitive issue. Apart from environmental "sticks", there was also an example of the more typical "carrot" approach, which in this case was based on a supplier environmental performance award.

Two companies mentioned that, despite the emergence of the so-called green consumer, customers were not always ready for more environmentally more friendly products. The two companies illustrated the danger of "jumping the gun" through the example of two products, a detergent and a paint, which were developed and marketed several years ago. Neither product sold and were taken off the market, only to be reintroduced recently when the companies judged the market to be ready.

Some respondents stressed the fact that senior management had adopted an internal policy not to include or use the environment in advertising, despite the fact that some companies explicitly stated that the environment had become a highly relevant competitive issue.

2.1.16 Technology and R&D

A few of the companies visited explained that new products must first pass through a "green" filter, during which they are exposed to a kind of TPLCA matrix with a point system, and/or submitted to a cradle-to-grave analysis. One company (a small firm) said that both the designer, production technicians and environmental specialists had an equal say in the development of new products. Some of the representatives of LEs in the study had assigned special R&D staff to focus on environmental issues related to their technologies. Research being carried out on environmental issues included:

- the greenhouse effect/global warming;

- water treatment;

- alternative power technologies; and

- alternative treatment of liquid effluents.

To some degree these R&D activities strongly reflect the line of business these companies are in.

2.1.17 Relations and/or communication with external stakeholders

It became clear during the study that many of the companies surveyed used various approaches to establish a dialogue with external stakeholders. The approaches reported in this study include:

- participation in various national and international environmental committees and business chambers;

- the establishing of an environmental hotline for customers and/or the general public;

- the use of lobbyists in Brussels;

- having regular round table discussions with the local neighbours;

- publishing and distributing environmental newsletters to the general public;

- open days;

- invitations to ad hoc press conferences;

- establishing an environmental liaison panel between the company and consumer representatives; and

- public attitude surveys.

Our general impression is that several of the companies surveyed have a good, constructive relationship with the authorities, and that an open and frank attitude is vital. But there was also criticism, indicating that it is becoming increasingly hard to keep ahead of environmental legislation, or that local environmental regulators have different standards in different regions.

Several of the companies have disclosed environmental information, primarily qualitative, since the early 1990s. Issues reported covered:

- mass balance sheet;

- costs of running the environment department;

- donations to environmental groups; and

- internal environmental performance indicators.

More than 30% of the companies reported bad news, and most of them both qualitatively and quantitatively. However, only 65% of these companies provided details of planned actions to deal with the problems. There are no discernible national differences in this area, but as regards industrial sectors, the electronics industry seems to behave a bit better than other industries.

One company visited had signed the Public Environmental Reports Initiative (PERI) and several companies were involved in more structured business environmental organisations and joint activities, such as:

- the Business Council for Sustainable Development;

- participation in international business environment conferences;

- the ICC Business Charter for Sustainable Development;

- the Responsible Care Programme;

- BAUM; and

- sponsorship of external environmental education-related projects and/or charity trusts.

One company organizes two-day seminars at business schools every year to share some of their experiences with environmental management.

Finally, the company visits revealed a couple of very interesting externally-oriented training initiatives. Thus, two of the companies have developed a package of teaching materials which they have distributed to an impressive number of secondary schools (18,000), while a third company is considering a similar initiative covering both primary and secondary schools.

2.1.18 Use of external consultants

The majority of the companies interviewed did not often make use of environmental consultants, and when they did, it was mostly for specialised scientific tasks, e.g. developing and implementing quality and environmental management systems.

One of the respondents mentioned the problem of finding consultants with sufficient knowledge of company operations and culture as one of the reasons for this. It was evident that LEs had more internal expertise than smaller companies.

2.1.19 Future expectations

Several respondents had some interesting expectations for the future. In general, it is expected that, concurrent with the gradual integration of the environment into all business functions, there will be fewer specialised departments for environmental management. As one respondent indirectly argued, the closer the organisation came to environmental sustainability (and he believed his company would become sustainable in the future), the less it needed an environment department and coordinator.

More companies provided details of environmental policy than disclosed their future plans for implementing it. Surprisingly, however, a majority of 15 companies now gave both qualitative and quantitative information, and 3 companies supplied quantitative information, whereas only 7 companies gave only qualitative information (see figure 2.7).

Figure 2.7. Information on future plans

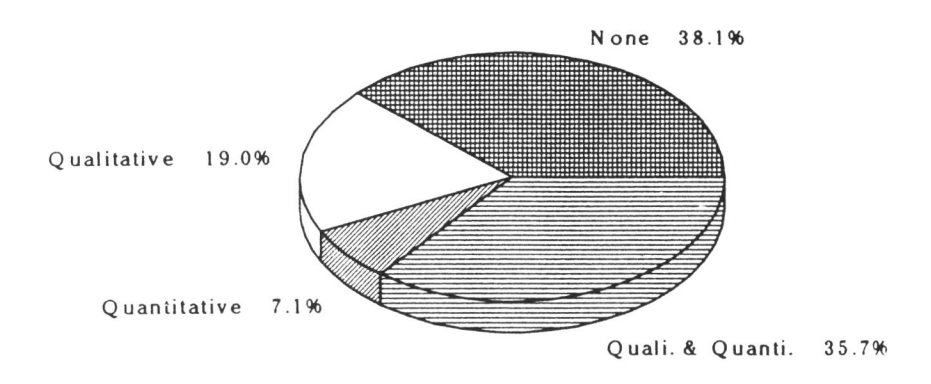

- None 38.1%
- Qualitative 19.0%
- Quantitative 7.1%
- Quali. & Quanti. 35.7%

The three biggest reporters of future plans for implementing environmental policy are identical with the major contributors to this survey: France, Germany, and the UK. Regarding industrial sectors, the chemical sector and the electronics sector are now both well represented, and, to a large extent, quantitatively.

The areas included in the analysis of future plans for implementing environmental policy were:

• air emissions (7 companies provided qualitative information, 5 quantitative, and 7 both);

• effluents (6 companies provided qualitative information, 5 quantitative, and 6 both);

- waste management (9 companies provided qualitative information, 5 quantitative, and 5 both);

- energy conservation (9 companies provided qualitative information and 5 both qualitative and quantitative);

- legislative compliance (3 companies provided qualitative information and 4 both qualitative and quantitative);

- supplier performance (6 companies provided qualitative information and 1 both qualitative and quantitative);

- product design (11 companies provided qualitative information and 2 both qualitative and quantitative);

- employee involvement (8 companies provided qualitative information and 2 both qualitative and quantitative);

- environmental management systems (10 companies provided qualitative information and 4 both qualitative and quantitative);

- environmental audit & disclosure (7 companies provided qualitative information and 3 both qualitative and quantitative); and

- sustainable development (4 companies provided qualitative information).

As can be seen, there is a varying degree of information concerning future plans in the individual areas. The most detailed and quantitative information is found under "air emissions", "effluents", and "waste management". For the remaining areas, the information is mainly qualitative. The structure is shown in figure 2.8.

The number of areas reported by the individual companies was fairly uniformly distributed. While no company reported on all 11 areas, 3 reported on 10 areas. The modal value is, however, 3-4 areas.

UK companies are again well represented regarding details of future plans, but again the information is often quantitative. French companies are close behind, whereas German companies mainly report qualitative information, and generally at a lower level. With regard to industrial sectors, chemical companies include a considerable number of details under "air emissions", "effluents", "waste management" and "legislative compliance" areas. Under "energy conservation", "consumer goods" and "power generation & distribution" companies are at the same level as chemical companies. There are no special tendencies in the remaining areas, except for "product design", where companies in the chemical sector provide a substantial amount of qualitative information.

Figure 2.8. Areas of implementation for future plans of environmental policy

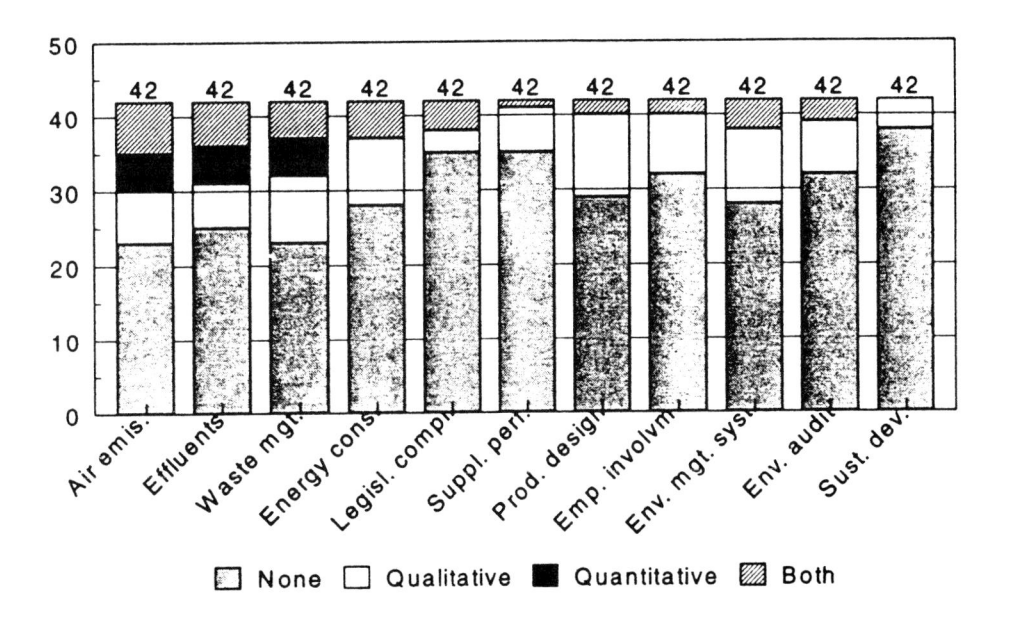

Other expectations noted include:

- increased standardisation of environmental management systems;

- more emphasis on recycling;

- more emphasis on business morals and ethics;

- LCA will be the (most) important quantification tool for future environmental management; and

- Europe's present role as the world's environmental opinion-former will be confirmed.

There were three other interesting exceptions. In two cases, the respondents did not believe that the other two pillars of sustainability should be left to politicians, since, they argued, companies had a definite role to play regarding poverty, and that, anyway, these were just starting to enter the business agenda. Another respondent argued strongly against this view, however, referring to a case where his company had refused to sign an environmental business charter because it also included other social dimensions, such as birth control. Another respondent argued that, in the future, science would no longer be accepted as the only voice on environmental issues.

2.1.20 Sustainability issues

Several visited companies expected more and more companies to gradually become more and more sustainable. The management of one of these companies had its own interpretation of the concept of sustainability: "To operate in such a way that you minimise your environmental impact on the Earth, not taking anything from the Earth that you cannot put back, thus operating in harmony with the planet".

2.1.21 Other observations

Complex processes and large companies are not the only ones with environmental impacts. One respondent also pointed to the necessity for looking at SMEs. In his country, it was estimated that up to 80% of VOC emissions were caused by SMEs. As another respondent argued that the problem with SMEs in this respect was their lack of money and expertise. Nevertheless, LEs can learn from SMEs and vice versa.

A number of other measures relating to operational activities were found in the study. These measures includes initiatives such as:

- refill services offered in all stores around the world;

- the use of recycling in all direct and indirect industrial processes;

- a plastic-box return system in use in European plants;

- materials marked with a code which refers to the material data;

- a take-back system for the reprocessing of plastic labels;

- a recycling system which recycles old car bodies, while newer cars are accepted for recycling free of charge;

- a huge energy project which aims at reducing the energy consumption of a whole island community by raising awareness and offering discounts on energy-saving techniques and methods; and

- a list of permitted chemicals for use in design and production.

2.2 CONCLUSION: CHARACTERISTICS OF EXISTING CORPORATE ENVIRONMENTAL MANAGEMENT PRACTICES

As previous experiences at the Department of Organisation and Management at the Aarhus School of Business have shown, large innovative companies also tend to be leaders in environmental management. In such companies, the greening process typically started more than one or two decades ago. The term "greening" should be used with caution, however, since there is a tendency in industry to include, for example, energy-saving measures from the 1970s under the umbrella of environmental management and concern. This, however, is open to debate.

Environment managers in environmentally leading companies have very different professional backgrounds, though mostly in technical and/or natural sciences. What is perhaps more interesting is the fact that none of them have been trained in environmental management. They are all "self-taught", though based on their existing degrees, of course.

The data describing the primary drivers give no single picture of the corporate greening process analysed in this study. Often, the process has started as a result of various combinations of internal drivers, e.g. cost reduction, and external drivers, e.g. environmental legislation. However, environmental legislation, customer demand and corporate image tend to be among the drivers most frequently mentioned.

The majority of interviewed companies expressed concern about several environmental problems. To a large extent, however, this only reflects the different lines of business of the individual companies. Many of the major corporate environmental problems mentioned were local in nature, although some companies did express a sincere concern for global and cumulative environmental effects, e.g. global climate change.

The findings regarding corporate values, objectives and strategies also present a complex picture. Many of the companies interviewed aim at surpassing existing environmental regulation, which indicates a strong need to become and/or remain proactive. The environmental policies analysed in this study address a huge number of specific environmental issues. Where an overall industrial environmental policy already exists, e.g. for the chemical industry, the companies included in this study typically apply and/or incorporate its guidelines.

Most of the companies visited already had some kind of environmental management system, although several did not ever expect to adopt BS7750 or EMAS, being wary of the bureaucracy and paperwork associated with such programmes.

Corporate environmental management activities are organised in different ways. The "classical" approach, also found in the study, is to let the environment manager coordinate and promote environmental policy. Actual policy implementation is handled jointly by the corporate environment manager and division and plant managers. Environmental responsibility thus rests with division and plant managers, not with the corporate environment manager.

Companies with a long history in safety and the working environment have typically established a Safety, Health and Environment Department, where environmental management issues are primarily handled. Such departments often act as a corporate advisory group, supporting and promoting a wide range of different projects. Another approach has been to form an Environmental Council or an Environmental Steering Group or Committee, consisting of key managers from various departments (and, in a couple of cases, external environmental authorities), to review progress and policy on environmental matters. This may be supplemented by various kinds of working groups and/or cross-functional management working teams to take care of specific problems and to create a forum for discussion.

In LEs, the strategic aspects of environmental management are usually the responsibility of the president, VP, or environment manager, whereas the operational managerial functions are often heavily decentralised.

The analyses revealed that environment managers, having direct access to the Board of Directors (if not the CEO), tend to exert a high degree of influence on corporate policy and strategy (and thus development).

Most of the corporate environmental information analysed in this study has been qualitative in nature. Quantitative information was also reported in a few cases, however, including mass balances and/or quantitative goals, and other performance indicators have been published. A number of companies intended to develop such indicators in the near future (presumably in the form of eco-balances or LCAs).

Many of the companies analysed here employed environmental audits or reviews. Such activities have normally been carried out for internal reasons, and in several cases they were carried out regularly. There are some indications that such activities can be expected to serve external/public interests, too, provided that disclosures can be made without seriously damaging corporate competitiveness.

The above examples of environmental management rely heavily on the ability to gather, process, and store environment-related data and to ensure easy access to such data by the "right" employees. Such systems were found in several of the companies visited.

Even the best environmental values and intentions are of little value if they are not translated and integrated into existing financial assessments and allocation procedures. Owing to the difficulty of separating environmental costs from other costs, among other things, it has not been possible to find any company with specific budgetary allocations and/or financial evaluation procedures for environmental activities and investments. In a few cases, environmental investments were not even submitted for "traditional" financial performance evaluation.

Several of the environment managers interviewed mentioned the importance of the support of all corporate employees. Employee commitment was encouraged by means of a multitude of approaches, of which internal training was frequently mentioned as being extremely important. Several internal channels of information were used to facilitate and/or speed up the level of employee awareness, most of which were updated and distributed regularly.

The earliest recorded corporate environmental training activities, which are mostly aimed at middle management downwards, date back to the early 1980s. The majority are of fairly recent date, however. Most of these training activities have been developed and carried out using internal resources. The various teaching approaches used range from "traditional" one-way approaches to interactive and participative forms and distance learning. Other companies have developed training courses for their suppliers in order to ensure a higher degree of compliance with internal environmental standards. In yet other cases, corporate teaching activities have also included external stakeholders such as schoolchildren.

The environment manager is often required to be a generalist. Many respondents sent a very clear message to future managerial educators and institutions to the effect that environmental issues must be fully integrated into all existing disciplines and courses. A basic understanding of the relationship between the economic and the natural system was called for, especially in traditional business economics curricula.

Some indications found in this study support the notion that the larger the company, the more heavily involved it is in environmental management issues. This should come as no surprise, however, since these companies typically have the financial, human and other resources needed for this. This can be seen from the analysis of corporate environmental R&D activities, which include research into more general environmental problems, such as global warming and alternative power technologies.

The majority of companies visited had a constructive and generally positive relationship with important external stakeholders, such as local environmental regulators and neighbours.

Regarding the future, several companies were optimistic that many of the existing trends in environmental legislation, environmental R&D, and the development of environmental management tools would become more widespread in the near future. A couple of companies also expected gradual corporate commitment to the other important pillars of sustainability (poverty, population growth, and the distribution of wealth).

3.0 EXAMPLES OF ENVIRONMENTAL MANAGEMENT PRACTICES

3.1 INTRODUCTION

The following section includes four examples of environmental management responses, which illustrate a few of the various aspects of corporate environmental management. The companies are not mentioned by name because it is the practice and characteristics of the environmental management initiative that are of interest here not the identity and history of the company concerned.

The first example focuses on the organisation of environmental issues and the structure of the environmental department in a large multinational service company. The second example describes how another company defined its environmental responsibilities into one vision and how this has influenced the environmental education and training of its employees. The third example illustrates the general approach to environmental management of a large multinational company, including policy, responsibility, environmental standards, drivers of environmental development, and key improvement areas. The fourth and last example describes how environmental performance is communicated to company stakeholders and how one company has tackled this issue by developing an environmental communication strategy.

3.2 EXAMPLES OF ENVIRONMENTAL MANAGEMENT RESPONSES

3.2.1 Example 1: Managerial and organisational approaches to corporate environmental improvement

This company is in the transport industry (people and goods), and employs 49,000 people worldwide.

In view of the increasing public interest in environmental issues and changing public perceptions of business-environment relationships, the company felt the need for an environment manager, a clearly-formulated environmental policy and an environmental organisation.

One of the company's seven corporate goals is to be a good neighbour to the local community and protect the environment. It defines community as the area surrounding the company's activities, but since it is both a local and a worldwide operator, this definition has been extended to include global communities. Based on this goal, the company has developed an environmental policy which, in its essentials, tries to meet the operational demands of the company without having a negative impact on the environment.

The company has developed a management and organisation programme to implement its environmental policy, including environmental reviews at the local and global level. Environmental reviews enable the company to assess the impact of its activities on the surrounding environment and community, and, in addition, help it to find possible solutions to problems. As a result of these reviews, a report containing various critical details is circulated to a limited number of managers. This is followed by an action list, identifying those areas that need to be worked on, by whom, and when. The action lists are distributed to the relevant operational staff. Finally, a summary report is distributed to staff, management, and other interested parties, particularly in the region in question. These reviews are just one way of identifying environmental problems, strengths, weaknesses, and opportunities within various functional areas. Outside consultants were used at first, because the environment department lacked the necessary resources, but now the reviews are carried out using both in-house expertise and consultants.

The environmental organisation is shown in figure 3.1.

Figure 3.1. The Environmental Organisation

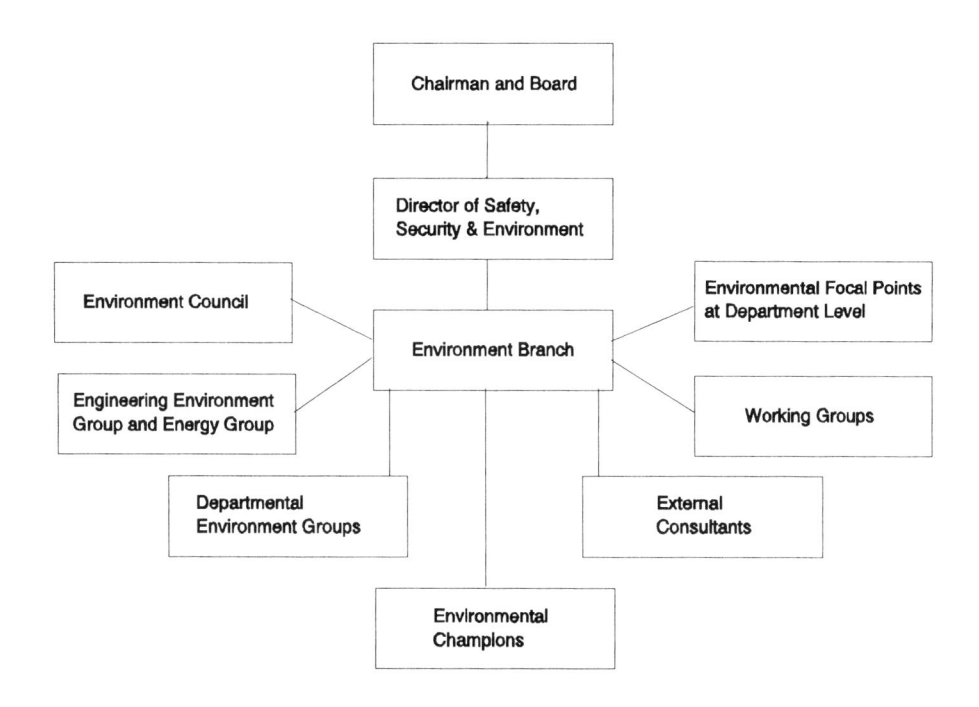

```
                    ┌─────────────────────┐
                    │  Chairman and Board │
                    └──────────┬──────────┘
                               │
                    ┌──────────┴──────────┐
                    │ Director of Safety, │
                    │ Security & Environment│
                    └──────────┬──────────┘
                               │
┌──────────────────┐           │          ┌──────────────────────┐
│ Environment      │───┐       │       ┌──│ Environmental Focal Points│
│ Council          │   │       │       │  │ at Department Level  │
└──────────────────┘   │┌──────┴──────┐│  └──────────────────────┘
                       └┤ Environment ├┘
┌──────────────────┐    │   Branch    │   ┌──────────────────────┐
│ Engineering Env. │────┤             ├───│  Working Groups      │
│ Group and Energy │    └──────┬──────┘   └──────────────────────┘
│ Group            │           │
└──────────────────┘           │
                               │
┌──────────────────┐           │          ┌──────────────────────┐
│ Departmental     │───────────┼──────────│ External             │
│ Environment Groups│          │          │ Consultants          │
└──────────────────┘           │          └──────────────────────┘
                    ┌──────────┴──────────┐
                    │   Environmental     │
                    │   Champions         │
                    └─────────────────────┘
```

Source: The company's environmental report

The Environment Branch is placed under the Director of Safety, Security & the Environment, who is responsible to both the Chairman and the Board of Directors. The Environment Council consists of employees from most functional areas, and is responsible for reviewing progress and policy in environmental matters. The Environmental Focal Points is a priority-giving system for senior management that is intended to cover the whole organisation. The Working Groups deal with various cross-company environmental issues, such as noise, waste, and recycling.

Environmental Champions are people who, with the approval of their managers, work for the improvement of environmental performance within their own department. One of the most important roles of the corporate environmental champion is to initiate and take part in activities which contribute to the "good neighbour" policy mentioned above.

The Departmental Environment Groups focus on issues in, for example, customer service, purchasing, and information management, with two separate groups in the engineering and energy areas.

According to corporate management, the job of the environment department is to promote cooperation and prevent departments from "reinventing the wheel". Since it can be difficult to convince departments to spend time on environmental matters, the environment department provides both input and information about unpopular problems which "have their own inertia". Senior managers and board members have explicitly acknowledged the need for an environmental management which helps to convince departments to allocate time and resources to environmental problems.

Middle management has taken the longest to implement an environmental organisation. With so many responsibilities to begin with, introducing additional initiatives often puts middle managers between the devil and the deep blue sea. Having to communicate in two ways, both with the shop floor and senior management, often complicates issues for middle managers. However, this is somewhat alleviated by the generally high level of interest in the environment on the shop floor. According to company management, "the environment has proven to be the only subject, apart from perhaps community issues, where people are prepared to work on their own time".

In the future, the environment department is expected to be decentralised from the corporate group and reduced to a very limited number of employees. In time, it will be replaced by full-time representatives in the various departments. Ideally, line management would totally integrate environmental management as part of their activities, thus eliminating the need for specialists and a separate environmental function. However, this will not happen in the foreseeable future.

3.2.2 Example 2: Corporate responsibility and environmental education requirements

This company is a leading multinational corporation in the biological and chemical products industry. It has 90,000 employees operating in more than 60 countries.

One of the company's most significant initiatives is the corporate responsibility vision, which it is currently implementing all around the world.

This vision guides general and specific business strategy, and is intended to take the company into the 21st century. The vision is based on the company's belief that survival depends on three areas of corporate responsibility. The first area is *economic responsibility,* which focuses on the ability of the company to fulfil, and keep on fulfilling, the economic demands of company stakeholders. A long-term view is necessary in order to generate company growth and ensure the constant renewal of a balanced business structure. The second area involves *responsibility towards society.* This includes communicating openly about company performance and operations. It also demands that company products add to the quality of life. New R&D products, which play an important part in company activities and strategy, must be turned into commercial reality if the company is to survive, but at the same time it has to evaluate the risks and accept public debate and interest. The third area involves *environmental responsibility.* Products must be produced and used with minimum environmental impact, natural resources must be used as efficiently as possible, and waste in all forms has to be reduced.

These three areas are separate, but closely interrelated. It is impossible to focus on improvement in one area while ignoring it in the others.

The company's corporate vision is the basis for all its business strategies, and has led to the formulation of four overall corporate goals. The first one requires all divisions to make environmentally sound products, i.e. they must carefully weigh the benefits of the product against the potential risks. The second is to develop safe production processes by using the smallest possible amounts of harmful substances. The third is to carry out exhaustive analyses of production processes, enabling the company to identify risks and weaknesses early on and take the necessary precautions. The fourth is to ensure that measures are taken to treat unavoidable waste and dispose of it without harming the environment.

To help achieve these goals and assist managers in the implementation of required measures, the company has joined the Responsible Care programme, developed by the Chemical Manufacturers Association for the chemical industry. This programme provides principles and guidelines for "responsible" industry with respect to employees, neighbours, the environment, and other industries. Individual companies adopt the programme and adapt it to their own particular culture, conditions, needs and priorities. The programme is divided into six areas:

- guiding principles;
- codes and checklists;
- measurement indicators;
- communication;
- worker safety; and
- the protection of people and the environment.

The company has also declared its support for the ICC Business Charter for Sustainable Development, which consists of 16 principles covering almost every aspect of business operations. However, the Charter is not used in day-to-day environmental management because of the fear that it would seem artificial and opportunistic. Environmental management is best explained to employees by means of concrete examples rather than abstract charters and guidelines.

One result of the formulation and implementation of the corporate responsibility vision is that the company has recognised that environmentally sound production is not solely a technical solution, but also involves the behaviour of employees and management. Or, as one manager put it: "An enterprise is made up of individuals with a wide range of attitudes, opinions and experience. Individual thought and action is what gives the company its character - a certain way of doing things". Environmental education, through courses, seminars and training programmes, thus plays a major role throughout the company.

The company has held training sessions on safety and the environment at its plants for several years. General information on safety and environmental policy is provided to all employees, while each plant is responsible for holding training courses according to its specific needs. There are a wide range of specialised courses for chemists, R&D scientists, and engineers in production and development departments. These focus on process safety, installations, environmental management and technologies, and the development of environmentally-friendly processes. In 1992, special initiatives, including courses on risk analysis and the environmental safety of computer-operated plants, were taken in various countries. In general, several respondents stressed the need for training programmes to be flexible enough to allow them to be tailored to the needs and organisational level of the employees in question. In consequence they are often selective in the information chosen for individual courses. Likewise, the duration of the courses will vary. At company headquarters, and in general management training, the main emphasis is on improving the degree of environmental awareness. But environmental policy is also discussed, and managers are given the opportunity to consider in detail the balancing of environmental, social, and economic responsibilities.

3.2.3 Example 3: Practising general environmental management

Example 3 is a multinational corporation with approximately 300,000 employees worldwide and a turnover of USD 64.5 billion in 1992. Information technology hardware, software, and related services are produced at 43 production sites around the world.

The first written company policy on the environment was issued in 1967 and still forms the basis of corporate environmental policy, although individual plants set their own objectives. The policy is used as a minimum standard worldwide. At the start of the greening process, the main focus was on health and safety, but this has changed in recent years, and now the external environment is a separate function with its own budget and organisation.

Company representatives claim that, seeking competitive advantage, the company has always kept one step ahead of environmental legislation in the area. But today's legislation is changing faster and in more areas than the company can cope with, and legislative compliance is becoming the norm rather than the exception. However, proactive monitoring of legislative changes and subsequent adaptation to them is still very often practised. For example, in anticipation of developments in European recycling and waste legislation, the company has begun to take back old discarded products and dispose of them under controlled conditions.

Overall environmental responsibility rests with the corporate environment vice-president, who defines the programmes, policies and standards to be implemented. The environment managers in the individual countries and plants around the world refer to the vice president. The company's environmental activities are documented, together with all aspects of environmental impact, in an environmental master plan. This plan is produced annually for every plant, and covers administration, external noise, protection of ground water, water, air, capital costs of environmental projects, emergency plans, and solid waste. To ensure compliance with corporate standards, the environmental plans are audited by environmental auditors. The auditing procedure includes financial as well as environmental auditing.

The main environmental impact of the company is through its products. Product stewardship has thus been recognised as one of the main environmental management challenges of the 1990s. Particular attention is paid to the following areas: (i) Raw materials. Recycling programmes have been initiated and product and component size reduced; (ii) Lowering energy consumption, reducing harmful emissions, and treating effluents; (iii) Packaging. The need for packaging is reduced by making the product smaller and more robust and packaging materials are either recycled or recyclable; (iv) Transport requirements, which are minimised by reducing the size and number of components. Furthermore, increased product reliability has reduced the number of service visits needed; (v) The most obvious environmental impact during a product's lifetime is energy use, but noise and emissions are also present. All these impacts have been reduced in new products; (vi) Disposal. More environmentally-friendly disposal involves reusing or recycling the product. In newer products the company has achieved 95% recyclability.

The company is currently considering EMAS and BS 7750 as a means of further systematising environmental management. According to the company, one of the most interesting differences between European and American managers lies in their views and attitudes towards environmental management systems. European managers often have a more positive attitude towards environmental management systems than their American counterparts.

Environment managers are the drivers of environmental development in most areas of the company. While the workforce has initiated some changes, there have been some problems with regard to changing habits, working routines and redistributing scarce economic resources. Employees are motivated to take the environment into account mostly through monetary incentives and by the communication of environmental information. The information is distributed through internal magazines and newsletters. In addition, all employees have access to electronically distributed information. Monetary incentive schemes range from individual employee prizes to national and plant awards. Another initiative is the development and implementation of an environmental training strategy. An external survey identified four functional groups in need of environmental education: employees in the marketing function, the design function, purchasers, and employees connected with environmental management. In the company's view, the technical part of environmental management can be taught, but the business part can only be learned from examples and working experience. The importance of a highly qualified workforce must never be underestimated. "You can have all the principles and policies in the world, but it's people who make them a working reality" is how one manager put it.

The company sees two areas as the key to improving environmental performance. One is the recycling of PVC, since this is the main material used in the manufacture of the company's products. Recycling loops have been developed and installed, and new ways of processing and moulding PVC to minimise waste have been implemented. The other area is company activities in information technology (IT). IT has obvious potentials for reducing industrial environmental impact. One example is a computer programme which enables the company's employees to log in to any work station when they are in the office. This has led to the more efficient use of office buildings, and has halved the number of office locations required in three years, thus saving space and energy.

It is company policy not to use the environment in advertising. The company discloses environmental performance information through environmental reports and publications, but will not sell its products based on the argument that they are relatively less harmful to the environment than some other similar product.

The knowledge acquired through environmental management is used to help customers and suppliers to minimise their own environmental impacts. Suppliers are required to adopt the same environmental standards as the company itself. At present, all suppliers and contractors are being surveyed to determine whether they live up to the company's standards and are suitable as future partners. It is becoming more and more apparent that the knowledge and expertise gained from environmental management is a valuable by-product of being in the forefront of corporate greening. In the past, such knowledge has been made available free of charge to suppliers and customers, but is now generally sold as an additional service of the company - in fact it could be seen as a new market for the company.

3.2.4 Example 4: Communicating environmental performance

This company is a metal recycling plant. It collects and recycles 500,000 tonnes of iron and metals into steel products. It has 1500 employees, and 70% of production is exported.

In the late 1980s, the company had major problems with environmental groups and local authorities, due to, among other things, dioxine emissions from the steel plant and a number of other environmental impacts. This also brought the company to the attention of the media and into the public debate on the environment.

In the past, environmental communication had received a rather low priority, and there were few attempts to seek a dialogue with environmental groups, the media, neighbours, etc., on environmental matters. As a result, the company was judged primarily on information from outside sources, which often gave a rather one-sided view of the issues.

Once they had recognised this problem, the company's management decided to improve environmental communication by, for example, changing the company's environmental image from a closed one to an open one. This resulted in the reorganisation of the company, with environmental issues being handled in a separate functional part of the technical department.

The company describes this renewal process as moving from a reactive stance to a proactive one. The company now considers itself to be the leading, i.e. the cleanest, steel company in Europe as regards the environment, and maybe even in the world.

An environmental accounting and reporting system is at the heart of the company's environmental information collection and performance evaluation. The system collects information about the resource use and environmental impacts of the production process and products, and distributes the information in various media. The system is intended to be the basis for "an objective discussion about how the environmental impacts resulting from company activities can be reduced further".

The 1991, 1992 and 1993 annual reports contain an input/output description of the production process for the year in question. All substances are registered in their basic form (e.g. Mn, Al, Pb, Sb, etc.), and reported in tonnes for substances and watts for energy. Instead of reporting the results in the usual columns of numbers, the company has chosen a graphic presentation form, where inputs are shown on the left, the production processes in the middle, and outputs on the right. A basic diagram for an input/output description is shown below in figure 3.2.

In addition, there are 6 "trend-graphs", where current environmental performance is compared with past performance. The six areas are: reused by-products; noise emissions; dust and particle emissions; heavy metals in received scrap; dust and particle concentration; and accident statistics. The information used in the input/output reports is audited, and the reports contain a verification statement by independent auditors. In the future, the report will continue to be published using mainly the same approach, with a mass balance sheet and trend curves as the focal points.

Figure 3.2. The basic structure of an input/output description

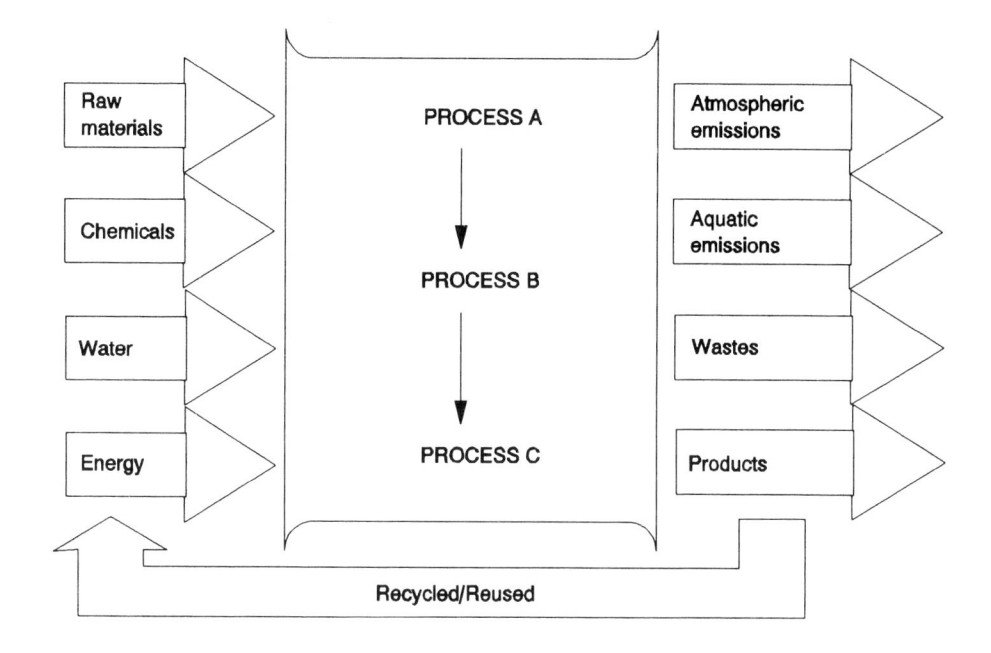

In a new initiative, the 1993 report also contains an "environmental declaration", describing the net environmental impact of one tonne of steel produced by the company. The declaration shows energy inputs measured in kWh, m^3 and kilograms, air emissions (with a focus on dust), heavy metals and CO_2, water use measured in m^3, emissions of heavy metals to waterways, by-products created during production measured in kilograms, number of accidents, number of accident-related absences, concentration of dust and heavy metals measured in $\mu g/m^3$, and lastly, the reuse percentage of by-products.

Another step in the communication strategy is the publication of environmental news in the internal newspaper, which is issued ten times a year. This is distributed to all national and local papers in Denmark, as well as to neighbours, customers and employees. The plant's neighbours are considered to be a very important source and recipient of information on environmental issues. This stakeholder group has to accept the company if it is to function in the local community, so it is vital to know what is going on. To ensure this, the company holds annual meetings with the local authorities on environmental issues. The company also has regular meetings with the regional authorities.

In communicating environmental issues to employees, the use of written media, such as internal newspapers, is not considered as important as direct communication by line managers. In the view of the company representative, the essence of leadership is motivating employees through clear organisational goals and objectives. This has a greater motivational effect than monetary rewards - also where environmental performance is concerned. The introduction and explanation of goals and objectives to employees is thus one of the most important parts of the internal communication strategy.

4.0 ENVIRONMENTAL MANAGEMENT EDUCATION AND TRAINING INITIATIVES: STATE OF THE ART

4.1 TRAINING IN ENVIRONMENTAL MANAGEMENT

4.1.1 Institutions of higher education

The survey includes (40 in all, of which 17 were interviewed) both new and old and small and large institutions of higher education and other training institutions offering full-time environmental management courses. The majority of institutions in the survey were small and new (less than 20 years old), however.

To give an impression of the variations in size, there were older institutions with more than 800 regular staff and 18,000 students, and small ones with no more than 15 full-time lecturers.

The majority of institutions visited and/or analysed offer graduate courses in environmental management or related issues, typically in normal and specialized courses. None of the "normal" institutions offering Master's degrees have integrated the environment into existing curricula, though some have implemented a more interdisciplinary strategy. It should be noted that, although offering courses in environmental management, including business issues, many of the institutions are not business schools.

Although the intention was to carry out a similar information material analysis for educational institutions as for companies, it was decided to limit the analysis to a more general description. The material received was neither extensive enough nor homogeneous enough to enable a more quantitative analysis, as in the case of the companies.

4.1.2 The respondent(s)

The respondents came from a wide range of professional backgrounds, including:

- economics and business administration;
- regional planning;
- psychology;
- sociology;
- manufacturing engineering;
- product engineering;
- agricultural science;
- philosophy;
- biology;
- chemistry; and
- mathematics and physics.

4.1.3 Drivers of sustainability in higher education

The existence of key external drivers of curricula greening was only vaguely acknowledged, indicating that the most important drivers were internal and/or personal (see below).

Among external drivers mentioned were:

- the increased visibility of environmental issues;

- social learning;

- public events (e.g. Earth day);

- international organisations, e.g. UNEP;

- public interest groups;

- competition from other universities and business schools;

- initiatives from pressure groups and the political system, plus media focus on the environment;

- population growth and the materialistic orientation of human needs;

- legislation on environmental impact assessment statements for power stations (this spurred the greening process in the institutions and the teaching of EIA methods and techniques, including the EIS procedure);

- recent EU environmental legislation has also motivated curricula greening; and

- the greening trend among local industry and authorities.

In practically all the institutions of higher education visited, the greening process had been started by individual internal environmental enthusiasts (professors), typically by developing training courses related to environmental management issues (bottom-up process). In one case, though, the original impetus came from the dean (top-down greening process).

4.1.4 Environmental courses offered

The institutions analysed in this report offer a wide variety of environment-related courses, both in scope and depth. In the following, a list of all the different types of environmental management courses offered will be given. A structured presentation of the information given below according to country and type of education can be found in annex 10. The breakdown of the courses is meant only as an aid to facilitate the reader, and should not be seen as an attempt at comparison or generalisation, since the information available is neither representative nor sufficient enough for this purpose. The majority of the courses are optional (electives), and form part of studies leading to a degree in areas other than the environment. Combined with the knowledge and experience from their main area of study, these courses provide the students with relevant qualifications in environment-related issues . Each number refers to an individual institution. Six of the institutions contacted are not mentioned since they only have research activities.

Austria

1. All business administration and economics students at this Austrian business school have to follow two environmental courses, one on the environmental underpinnings of business and the other on business in its social and ecological environment. Courses offered at Master's level are ecology, resource and environmental economics, risk management and risk communication, environmental law, environmental management, and environmental strategies. The school also offers seminars on environmental technology, environmental management, and environmental ethics.

Denmark

2. The 27-month course at this Danish business college has a theoretical

and a practical part, and focuses on educating economists with a technical and environmental background. The first part gives a general introduction, and is followed by a trainee period. At the end of this period, specific aspects of company-environment relationships are discussed, interspersed with additional trainee periods. Specifically, the course focuses on environmental law, environmental technology, biology, ecology, wastes, cleaner technology, economics, investment, finance, marketing, purchasing, organisation, and environmental pollution.

3. Recycling and pollution prevention, environmental industrial techniques. An experimental Master's course in Environmental Management is offered at this Danish university, mostly to engineering students. The courses are offered during the last 3 semesters and include: water purification techniques, cleaner technology, resource economics, environmental law, microbiology, statistics, hydrology, microbe ecology, environmental regulation and planning, ecotoxicology, air pollution, soil, and the working environment.

4. Two courses in LCA techniques for engineering students at this Danish technical university. The first, which is offered to first-year civil engineering students, is a general introduction to the LCA concept. The second is offered in the sixth semester, and is more detailed.

5. The existing collaboration between this Danish university's Faculty of Technical Science and Faculty of Social Science includes separate courses on the environment and economics. Students are then required to combine the two in their projects. A green MSc started in 1994 in collaboration with the Faculty of Business. The main focus is on environmental management problems and management approaches to environmental problems, though the curricula are not finished. There

are two other possible combinations: One combines environmental education with teacher training, and is mainly aimed at adult education. The other combines environmental education with the developing countries. A PhD course in sustainable EM started in 1994.

6. This Danish business school offers three environment-related Master's courses (each course 2 hours a week for 6 months), focusing on corporate EM, the relationship between the economy and the environment, the relationship between consumer behaviour and the environment, and the relationship between business strategy and the environment. The courses involve work on assignments and active participation in the classes. A PhD programme in continuation of these three courses started in early 1995.

7. A 1-year Danish interdisciplinary course, focusing on biology, environmental medicine, chemistry, geology, humanities, and the social sciences, including economics. The course is aimed at all university graduate students close to finishing their degree.

England

8. Six courses are offered in different areas at this English university: (i) the environmental agenda for management development, (ii) the green opportunity, (iii) developing greener products, (iv) the green challenge to R&D, (v) environmental audit, (vi) green policies add to the bottom line. A new MSc started in 1994. The structure will consist of 8 modules, of which 6 are core modules. There are also 12 executive environmental management courses.

9. Courses in Environmental Economics are offered to business and economics students at this English business school.

10. An environmental MSc has been developed and prepared (at the time of visit) at this English university. In addition, four social accounting courses and two courses in environmental management are offered, both at undergraduate level. There are ten lectures over a period of 14 weeks.

11. An environmental MBA offered from 1994 at this English university. There are four core modules and a specialized module in eco-management, with room for 30 students. The MBA is aimed at people with practical experience in environmental management. The first half focuses on defining the problems and challenges of environmental issues and the company-environment relationship. The second half is centred around strategy and company relations to local and regional economies, change management, and EA. The main aim is to connect environmental management to local and regional aspects when solving company-related environmental problems.

12. Two executive courses on the marketing of chemicals in a greener world and the role of environmental issues in strategic planning, and one MBA course on EM, focusing on the background of environmental issues, legislation, and environmental management tools and their use. In addition, 10% of one course on corporate responsibility is devoted to environmental issues. This institution is an English business school.

13. This English university offers environmental planning, an MSc programme in environmental assessment and management, mostly for students of the natural sciences. This new MSc has 35 students, and focuses on methods and procedures for EIA and EM from a British and EU perspective. There are also specialized undergraduate modules in environmental planning, which focus on the use of information from EA, EIA and EM systems. There are plans for an MSc in EA

together with the school of business. Offers tailor-made training packages for companies on the EMAS.

14. Two courses offered at this English business school: 1. Corporate environmental strategy (environmental strategy, the physical environment, environmental capacity, systems management, and environmental risks); 2. Environmental management and auditing.

15. The postgraduate and graduate courses offered at this English university include: ecology, environmental control and public health, environmental policy in an international context, physical resources and the environment, and the enterprise and the environment, which focuses on the company's relationship with the physical environment (legislation, awareness, standards, new product development, waste, HRM, audits). Also offered are study packages on environmental issues for specialists and managers. Distance learning packages on environmental issues for SME managers are also in the pipeline.

16. This English university postgraduate course includes: (i) Business and the environment, which mainly discusses the social aspects of environmental management and is concerned with integrating management and environmental objectives; (ii) Biodiversity and sustainable resource development (expected to begin in 1995); (iii) Tourism, conservation, and sustainable development; (iv) Diploma in environmental management and business: a distance learning programme suitable for those wanting a business administration qualification with environmental aspects; (v) Diploma in ecology, conservation and environmental management: a part-time, two-year course.

France

17. Courses in Environmental Economics are offered to business and economics students at this French university.

18. Two courses offered at this French business school for 12-15 students each, one on industrial ecology and industrial metabolism and the other on the management of environmental resources. 16 lectures and discussion classes. The school also offers a three-day executive development programme on sustainable environmental strategies.

19. This French university offers a one-year course specializing in environmental engineering, drawing on the expertise of 83 different teachers and 38 different organisations. Applicants have different backgrounds, but nearly all come from the natural or technical sciences and have plans for a career in environmental management. Courses offered include environmental economics, environmental communication, the cleaning-up of environmental pollution, and ecology.

20. This French university offers a MSc course in community planning and urban environmental planning.

Germany

21. Short-term (1-2 days) courses offered at this German postgraduate training institution focus on a single environmental issue, such as waste management, environmental communication, etc. A special course on the EMAS scheme is also available. In addition, there are courses of longer duration, up to 8 months, which are aimed at natural scientists and technicians training in environmental management (the course includes communication, organisation, accounting, finance, etc.). The course explores general and technical

environmental issues in relation to the company and the legislative background. Entrance requirements to the course are a university degree or documented relevant practical experience.

22. This German university offers a 3-semester course in environmental economics. 1st semester: the relationship between man and nature, economy and nature. 2nd semester: market failures, growth-environment conflicts, environmental law. 3rd semester: relations to business management. In addition, there are various postgraduate conferences and workshops.

23. This German university's Business Faculty offers 7 subject areas for the final degree in business administration, one of which is EM. More than 100 economics students follow the course, 30 of whom are especially active. The number of courses and seminars varies from semester to semester.

24. This German university offers a specialized course in environmental management (the last two of 8 semesters). The course discusses five issues: Strategic EM and Eco-control, EM as a part of other management functions, environmental policy, environmental law, and environmental ethics.

25. A "block" of four basic courses is offered at this German university: Ecology and environmental technology, environmental law, environmental planning, and the shortcomings of the market allocation mechanism. Also offered is a specialized course in environmental economics, focusing on policy instruments, measurements, and coordination problems. Another specialized course, in environmental management, focuses on environmental planning, instruments, risk, labelling, etc.

26. German short-term postgraduate university courses offered (12-25 participants) include eco-balances and eco-controlling, eco audits and environmental auditing in the EU, and environmental marketing.

27. A German university specialized course in environmental economics, with a focus on the environment-economics relationship, control, policy, instruments, and German environmental policy and control, etc.

Switzerland

28. A two-year postgraduate specialized course in environmental management is offered at this Swiss training institution. Year 1: (i) Basic courses in ecology, chemistry, mathematics, etc.; (ii) Ecosystems and their protection. Year 2: (i) Basic courses (environmental ethics, environmental economics, human ecology, ecology and the company); (ii) Environmental hygiene; (iii) Environmental protection in densely populated/intensely used areas.

29. Apart from the more natural science-oriented environmental courses offered at this Swiss university, there are also courses on environmental ethics and environmental economics, the company and the environment, market-based instruments for environmental protection, risk analysis, and the man-nature relationship over the last 50 years.

The Netherlands

30. An environmental MBA degree, including three environmental electives (EM, environmental policy, waste management), and two special workshops (sustainable development and environmental communication), is offered at this Dutch business school, involving teachers from three European countries.

31. This Dutch training institution offers two nine-week postgraduate courses in environmental management in industry, and safety, health and environmental management.

32. A one-year course for MSc or MA graduates in environment-related disciplines, focusing on environmental science and environmental problem-solving, environmental policy, and environmental tools. The course is aimed at graduates who aspire to a professional career in managerial and policy-making positions. The course is a joint project between two Dutch universities.

33. Three specialized environmental courses at this Dutch university: Master of environmental business administration (full-time): (i) basic courses (4 months), case projects (4 months), and traineeship (2 months). Participants are trained in developing environmental management systems for industrial organisations; (ii) Public environmental management (full-time): basic courses (5 months), case projects (1 month), and traineeship (4 months). This course covers: (a) integral branch-specific controls; (b) corporate environmental management and permits; (c) recent legislative developments; and (d) project management; (iii) Environmental consultancy (part-time): basic courses (4 blocks of 2 days), case projects (3 blocks of 3 days), and internal company training (3 months).

The variety of information given above reflects the variations in scope, intentions, and extension. Some of the institutions included in the study described their courses in detail, while others only sent a short leaflet containing the names of the courses. The most detailed information, of course, was obtained from the institutions which were visited and interviewed.

4.1.5 Teaching approaches and materials

Almost all the teaching approaches used in environmental management courses were based primarily on lectures and one-way communication. Most of the exceptions had small classes (≤ 25) and adopted approaches based on the active participation of the student. The various approaches included:

- interdisciplinary, problem- and project-oriented group work, where the students themselves are primarily responsible for defining and solving realistic problems; thus the teacher has mainly a consulting and guiding role;

- hands-on experience in real-life organisations;

- excursions;

- workshops;

- case studies;

- student presentations;

- negotiation exercises;

- role-playing games; and

- traineeship in companies.

The general impression is that there is a tendency to develop internal teaching materials, partly consisting of extracts from books and articles and partly of internally developed materials. In many cases, this was explained as being because of the general lack of relevant text material. The various types of materials included:

- textbooks;

- local papers;

- reference lists;

- local cases;

- video cassettes; and

- audio cassettes.

4.1.6 The role of EM educators and educational institutions

On the roles and responsibilities of environmental educators at institutions of higher education, it was stated that they should:

- teach theory, values and tools;

- enhance the understanding of natural complexities and system knowledge and team-building qualifications (rather than specific knowledge);

- provide holistic and pragmatic solutions to environmental problems;

- teach students to become agents of change; and

- discuss the strategic implications between man-made and natural systems.

Many respondents emphasized the need to train students to become generalists, and there was also a strong belief that educators must teach values, attitudes and norms, too.

The replies confirmed the role of environmental educators. Answers included:

- universities have an important role in setting the agenda for social change, though they should beware of adopting a "missionary" tone;

- they should produce reports which can influence political decision-makers;

- they should serve as initiators of new research and areas of interest;

- they should stay ahead of business and be ready to criticise the status quo;

- they should serve as creators and supporters of general social responsibilities; and

- they should have a role as important societal opinion-makers.

4.1.7 The ideal environmental education

There was widespread agreement that environmental issues should be integrated into all departments and at both Bachelor and Master level. One respondent went so far as to suggest that, ideally, it ought to be integrated at all educational levels, from kindergarten and upwards.

4.1.8 Barriers to the greening of curricula

As with the corporate greening process, both internal and external barriers to the process of educational greening were mentioned.

Examples of internal barriers:

- lack of qualified staff, i.e. professors with sufficient skills and knowledge of the area;

- resistance from colleagues;

- institutional inertia; and

- lack of priority.

External barriers included:

- resistance from the scientific community within the individual disciplines;

- lack of funds/difficulty in raising funds; and

- lack of student interest (reported in three cases!!).

As regards the latter, one respondent, representing one of Europe's leading MBA institutions, explained that many students from abroad still do not consider the environment as a stepping stone to a fast career (which is what they are normally aiming at).

4.1.9 Relations with business

Other initiatives mentioned, which further demonstrate the oft-reported very close relationship with industry, include:

- tailor-made courses for companies;

- sponsorship (in two cases, a chair);

- trainee positions; and

- specific assignments related to actual problems in companies.

4.1.10 Current and future research activities

The main impression from the institutions included in the study is that ongoing research activities in the area of business and the environment are largely unstructured and ad hoc, eschewing major cross-departmental and institutional cooperation.

Present research includes:

- cleaner technologies;

- urban ecology;

- energy and transportation;

- LCA methodology;

- ecological economics;

- international dimensions of environmental protection;

- regional development;

- waste management;

- industrial metabolism;

- material balances;

- full-cost pricing methods;

- green competitive opportunities;

- green accounting;

- environmental legislation;

- corporate environmental best practices;

- the relationship between the development of new technology and environmental performance;

- methods in environmental evaluation and performance measurement;

- risk analysis;

- wildlife conservation;

- environmental learning processes in government and industry; and

- scientific research, such as organic compounds.

Planned and/or expected future research activities include:

- integration processes;

- the effects of infrastructure on environmental management;

- new pollution abatement techniques;

- environmental management and company behaviour;

- material balance accounts;

- LCA;

- corporate environmental scanning;

- the monitoring of post-environmental development;

- the concept of sustainability; and

- the relationships between regulation and self-regulation.

4.1.11 General expectations for the future

There was general optimism among the respondents about the prospects for sustainable development. There was a wide range of expectations, including:

- environmental regulators will change from carrying out environmental policing to becoming "corporate environmental supervisors";

- the importance of environmental accounts and sustainability will increase;

- safety, health, environment and quality will merge;

- environmental training and education will become integrated into both undergraduate and graduate teaching in business schools; and

- in order to improve their ability to deal with related TQM, HRM, marketing and legislation issues, future environment managers can also be expected to have a non-technical background.

4.1.12 Other observations

One professor (a well-known authority and author on environmental auditing and management) was unsure as to whether the interest of his own field in environmental research was prompted by other considerations than it simply being a new area to explore. This fear may apply to other groups, too.

The future company model will be à la Body Shop. However, if sustainability is to be achieved, there will have to be a restructuring of the global economy and a critical review of the fundamental tenets of capitalistic society - i.e. materialism and consumerism.

One respondent said that the only way for schools to avoid having to reinvent the wheel was for the government to adopt a common framework for environmental education.

During the visits, a couple of professors called for shorter courses on environmental management for present corporate managers and postgraduates. Others pointed to the need for more feedback, both from students who have gone on to jobs in industry and from the business community itself.

Interdisciplinarity was a preference in two other cases. An interdepartmental research group with a special interest in business administration and sustainable development had been established at one of the business schools visited.

At another university, all research activities must be interdisciplinary, with at least two of the main sciences represented. Fund applications have to specify the interdisciplinarity of projects.

4.2 CONCLUSION: CHARACTERISTICS OF EXISTING MANAGEMENT EDUCATION

Up to now, little has been known about how managers with responsibilities for environmental affairs acquire their knowledge and expertise. During the past decades, it has become clear that industry's environmental responsibilities have grown with alarming speed, often threatening the very existence of companies faced with strong financial liabilities. By contrast, the education and training of future and existing managers has generally lagged behind, as this study has shown.

A recent UK study illustrated this gap in figures (UNEP, 1993). The study showed that 60% of the managers surveyed and working in UK companies had no environmental content in their basic qualifications. It was found that other educational methods than formal training courses were more often used (see figure 4.1).

Figure 4.1. UK environmental managers' methods of developing expertise

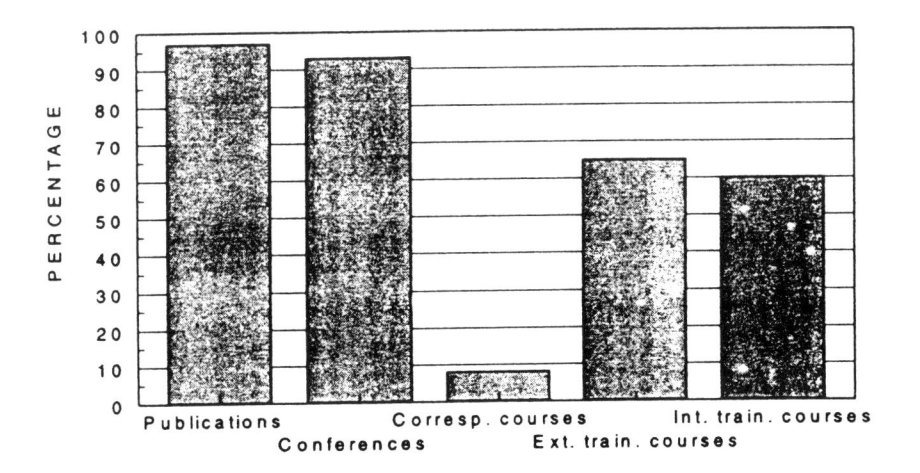

Source: UNEP (1993).

As this study indicates, however, there are some positive signs of change, and a growing emphasis on environmental education in business schools and other institutions of higher education (though still in a minority). A recent estimate suggests that about twelve European business schools have developed, or are developing, courses exclusively devoted to environmental management (Moser and Arnold, 1993).

During the 1990s, an increasing number of university presidents signed The Tailloire Declaration, which, among other things, calls for the creation of programmes to enable faculties to introduce environmental perspectives and values into all courses in order to produce future graduates who are environmentally literate and competent (Cortese, 1993).

And, as this study has shown, a number of LEs have begun to provide environmental training and educational programmes, both for their employees and their suppliers. One of the surveyed companies had even developed a total teaching package for secondary schools. Industrial organisations such as ICC and WICE have also established advisory and/or working groups on business education and training programmes.

The majority of institutions visited and/or analysed offer graduate courses in environmental-management-related issues, typically in specialized courses. None of the "normal" institutions offering a Master's degree have fully integrated the environment into existing curricula. In a few cases, a more interdisciplinary strategy has been implemented.

The key educators of environmental management in the selected sample represent a variety of professional backgrounds, none of which can be claimed to be "tailor-made" for the job. The various disciplines represented include the social sciences, the technical sciences, and the natural sciences, with a predominance of the first one.

The important drivers of the greening process at these institutions can be grouped into internal and external drivers. The most frequently mentioned driver, however, was that of the environmentally-dedicated teacher or teachers.

Whether owing to a lack of willingness to cooperate or lack of relevant activities, the quantity and quality of information provided varied quite a bit. The general impression from this part of the study supports the basic assumption that, in institutions of higher education, environmental concern and interest is best dealt with by means of an unstructured, non-integrated, ad hoc approach.

The institutions included in this study offer environmental courses at either undergraduate, graduate, or postgraduate level (in some cases, at all levels), typically as electives among other (relevant) choices.

A detailed analysis of the specific content and teaching approaches adopted in such management courses reveals some interesting characteristics. First, such courses typically have a limited number of students (up to, or less than, 25 students). Second, they are often based on interactive participation. Third, they have close contacts with local industry (students are often required to carry out their assignments in collaboration with local firms). Fourth, they are characterised by a multitude of teaching methods, only using the "traditional" one-way communication approach to a limited extent.

Most of the above-mentioned courses are of very recent date. This is partly because many of the present educators have had to develop their own teaching material since there is a lack of relevant textbooks in the field. One of the few available textbooks on environmental management by Welford & Gouldson (1994) has just been adopted by several of the educators.

The importance of educators' and institutions' roles and responsibilities in teaching values and attitudes was strongly emphasized. It was also stressed that institutions have both a very important political role to play and a role as opinion-makers.

The process of curriculum greening has not been allowed to proceed unimpeded. It has run up against various kinds of barriers, ranging from external barriers, such as scientific communities and the providers of research funds, to internal barriers, such as colleagues and (particularly for the older and larger institutions) institutional inertia.

Current research at these institutions is specialized and carried out in isolated research environments with none or very limited international cooperation. Furthermore, it tends to be ad hoc, both in the way it is carried out and in the way it is described, and seems rarely to be part of local major research plans and/or programmes. In fact, it was only possible to find (three) major planned and interdisciplinary programmes with international collaboration in one of the countries surveyed.

With regard to the future, respondents were generally optimistic that the greening process will increase.

5.0 EXAMPLES OF ENVIRONMENTAL MANAGEMENT EDUCATION AND TRAINING INITIATIVES

5.1 INTRODUCTION

The following section gives three examples of how educational institutions have responded to the call for environmental education. The examples show a few of the most interesting initiatives encountered. The institutions, like the companies in chapter 3, are not identified in the report for the same reason, i.e. it is the initiative itself, not the institution, that is of interest here.

The first example describes the characteristics of an interdisciplinary environmental course and the problems of organising and running it. The second example illustrates the efforts of one large university to develop an environmental MBA. The third, and last, example is of a course in environmental business economics, including both interdisciplinary courses and a trainee period in a company.

5.2 EXAMPLES OF EDUCATIONAL RESPONSES

5.2.1 Example 1: Training interdisciplinary environmental consultants

This institution was founded in 1987 as an independent non-profit organisation. Through a Community pilot scheme, it became involved in an educational project being tested in 50 municipalities aimed at promoting environment-friendly behavioural patterns. The aim of the initiators was to develop a very specific training programme for a very specific function, viz. the environmental consultant, which was lacking both in business, local authorities, and government. This type of function already existed in another country, albeit at a very unstructured level, but there was no similar course in the French educational system. After the pilot project, all participants agreed that this type of course was precisely what they had been looking for. Negotiations with universities and other institutions about possible collaboration proved fruitless, however; they were not interested in participating. In the end, the handful of people involved decided to go it alone. After the necessary preparations and research, they started on the first one-year training course. It is no exaggeration to say that the course has been a tremendous success. Up to now, over 200 environmental consultants have graduated, and last year there were 2000 applications for the 35 places. Students are hand-picked by means of personal applications, interviews and psychological tests. The management of the institution personally participates in the selection process, actively assisted by a psychologist and a number of former students.

During the first three years, the course was financed by EU funding and regional authorities. From 1992, students had to finance half the training course themselves, while the other half was still financed by the regional authorities. This financing form is the one used today, and is considered satisfactory.

The course itself takes one year full-time or two years part-time. Each new intake has to develop and define its own curricula and course contents. The course consists of 26 modules centred around six main topics: The environment, and biological, ecological and physical processes; sustainable development and the implications of the concept; communication, negotiation and dissemination; institutional and legal organisation regarding the environment; regional environmental planning and development; and tools and methods. The course has a strong regional focus - i.e. the environmental consultant is matched to the region he or she will be working in.

The course is divided into a 5-month theory term (35 teaching hours a week) and a 6-month practice term in a company or organisation. The practice term ends with the writing of a thesis. These are subsequently used as teaching material, and there are now 160 theses on various subjects which the institution can draw on. Likewise, students also develop their own specific tools, e.g. methods for measuring emissions and company environmental auditing methods. The methods developed by one class are often further developed by subsequent classes. For example, a methodology developed by one class is applied and tested by the next, and the following classes improve it. So far, the results of this teaching and research are only available to the environmental consultants themselves, but general publication is intended in the future. The institution has a very pragmatic way of evaluating the efficiency of the training - it simply asks the students. "Grab sessions" are held, where students have the opportunity to complain about everything to do with their education - the teachers, the content, the approach, as well as their fellow students. After 2 1/2 months of professional practice, during which they apply what they have been taught, they meet again to evaluate the training. Similarly, after graduation, they are asked for a written evaluation of the entire one-year course. Former students give feedback on the quality and applicability of the course in the jobs and positions they occupy.

Most of the students have a university education and are already specialists in various fields when they start the course. The biggest challenge to the students is the interdisciplinary and intercultural nature of the course. The students do not have the same way of thinking, and have different educational backgrounds and working experience. This is most clearly seen in the case of team work, where students specialized in different fields are placed in groups to solve various problems. The students have to seek assistance from each other, and they eventually learn who and which discipline to turn to in solving various types of environmental problems. They can also draw on this knowledge after graduation as this kind of training develops a strong network which survives long after the course is over. Thus, according to the respondents through this course a specialist "is turned into a well-communicating, visionary generalist serving sustainable development".

The majority of the environmental consultants are employed by local authorities. His or her function is generally to inform, to advise on, and to coordinate the environmental actions taken, and to develop an environmental plan. Many environmental consultants are employed by private companies as well. Companies located in highly industrialised urban areas need to improve their environmental performance if they want to stay there. Thus, the role of the environmental consultant is often to facilitate cooperation and communication between the various parties - local authorities, ministries, various government agencies, environmental groups, and other companies, etc.

Future planned improvements at the institution include increased technical assistance to students and environmental consultants, and an expansion of international activities, e.g. assisting Central and East European countries to establish their own environmental consultant education.

5.2.2 Example 2: Developing an environmental MBA programme

Located in a very large population centre, this university has over 18,000 students and 800 professional staff. Structurally, the university is divided into 6 centres, or educational institutions, each with their own faculties. One of the institutions is involved in environmental issues and "seeks to develop the student's potential and capability in the design, construction and management of the environment".

The environment centre is divided into three areas. The first focuses on the built environment, encompassing construction management, economics and technology, together with civil engineering and building and quantity surveying. The second is environmental management and design, which is further subdivided into environmental health (control of environmental quality) and urban development and housing (improvement in environmental quality). The third area offers professional and postgraduate courses in architecture, planning, and acoustics.

An MBA programme in environmental management has been established in cooperation with the faculty of business, offering MBA students a specialization in environmental management. The programme started in 1994, and was developed (curricula, cases and teaching materials) in collaboration with a German university. The structure of the course has drawn heavily on the extensive experience of the lecturers in environment-industry relations, and on discussions with students and private companies.

The main aims of the programme are, first, to provide an understanding of the key elements of the business-environment debate; second, to enable participants to introduce environmentally relevant changes into their own organisations; and, finally, to help students identify and participate in a wider approach to the environment within their local and regional communities.

The key topics addressed are:

- an introduction to environmental management, explaining the need for action on environmental matters, how they are related to environmental and economic systems, and the scale of the problems in business;

- the economic background of environmental problems, such as externalities, weaknesses in conventional economic systems, and sustainable economics;

- political, spatial and legal considerations relating to environmental issues, and the global-local debate and related problems concerning transnational regulations, loss of the commons, and the current and future structure of environmental legislation and its impact on firms;

- business organisations and the evolution of green thinking, including how the environment has been viewed by business in the past, and the development of total costing and corporate responsibility;

- the characteristics and nature of major environmental problems, their origin and how to contain them, as well as justice and equity;

- introduction to environmental auditing and assessment, the use of these tools in practice, introduction in firms, future developments;

- company organisation and behaviour, including the integration of the environmental management approach, how environmental management is incorporated into strategy and linked to implementation, and the concept of environmental management systems such as BS 7750, including the relationships with suppliers and customers;

- the costs and benefits of introducing environmental management, new markets, products and services, and the problems of full cost;

- the process of environmental management in business, including awareness-raising and the move to a new paradigm, as well as the consequences of not changing attitudes, and mechanisms for enforcement; and

- the challenge of change, the question of equity in sustainable development, the ever-changing nature of ecosystems, and the need for a dynamic approach to environmental management.

The environmental MBA programme is mostly based on lectures and workshops, which discuss important topics introduced in the lectures. The students themselves are responsible for the workshops.

Apart from a thesis, students will be assessed on case work - students select a particular topic and illustrate it by means of a company case study. The student outlines the nature of the problem, indicates the potential solutions, explains the actions taken by the company, and evaluates the outcome.

Research opportunities in environmental management consist of a number of research programmes and projects, leading to a PhD degree. Among the main areas of research are energy management, environmental assessment and auditing, strategic planning and management, and local and regional economic planning and development.

One area which receives much attention is the idea of relating environmental management to the local and regional economy, rather than focusing solely on standard solutions and methods. Solutions have to include regional differences and rely on regional expertise and networks. The cumulative environmental impact of small and medium-sized enterprises (SMEs) is just as important as that of large enterprises. The respondent suggested three themes which were likely to be important in future research in this area: (i) to identify forms of economic organisation which respect the environment and minimize impact; (ii) to identify spatial modes of social organisation which minimize environmental impact; and (iii) to combine the sectoral and spatial elements in an environmentally-balanced planning and regional development. The methods and approaches used in company environmental management should be adapted to local and regional differences, not based on the same standard approach. Successful environmental management is company-specific, and, to a large extent, dependent on the dynamic nature of the local and regional environment.

5.2.3 Example 3: Educating environmental business economists

This institution has initiated a 27-month full-time course called "The Environmental Business Economist", which started in Autumn 1993. The aim of the course is to enable students to analyse and report about problems which (in relation to the company's environmental initiatives) form the basis for economic decision-making, e.g. evaluation of the implementation of cleaner technologies, and the legal, logistical, and organisational aspects of environmental initiatives, etc. The aim is to give students trained in economics some technical and environmental knowledge. Although business graduates were the initial target group, applicants come from a variety of professional and educational backgrounds (e.g. environmental technicians and natural sciences), and, with an average age of 25, are also older than expected. Only half of the students have a business qualification. In general, students were very involved in environmental issues before they applied to the course, and are thus already very interested in the business-environment relationship. The selection procedure is based on conversations and personal applications, where applicants have a chance to talk about their reasons for applying and why they think the environment is an important part of business economics.

The course starts with a general introduction to environmental, economic and organisational issues, which prepares students for the subsequent trainee period. After the first trainee period, the course focuses on the more interdisciplinary and specific aspects of environmental management and control. Currently, 14 companies are participating in the training programme. These were screened carefully in advance to weed out companies just looking for cheap labour. In addition, the companies were required to sign a contract committing them to participation in the programme for the duration of the course. Generally, companies need to be of a certain size to be able to allocate the necessary time and resources to the trainees, although this is by no means required. The institution has full control over the trainee period, and gets feedback from the students about the companies plus feedback from the companies about the students and their qualifications and performance. During the trainee period, students come into contact with all aspects of the company's environmental activities, and meet all the different functions and persons who have an influence on the decision-making processes and the company's environmental performance. Students are also exposed to different organisational cultures and values, and hence gain experience in communicating with different functions about environmental issues. There are inherent conflicts in the environment-economy relationship, which cannot be solved by using macroeconomic methods in a microeconomic context. Students experience these at first hand during their trainee period, and can refer to them later in the theoretical part of the course.

The course can be roughly divided into an environmental part and a business economics part. The *environmental part* includes: (i) Environmental law (broad overview); (ii) Biological and ecological aspects of the environment, and the effects of various pollutants; (iii) Environmental technology (clean-up technologies for companies and society); (iv) Hazardous waste (definitions, laws, procedures, disposal, etc.); and (v) Cleaner technology (methods and procedures for tackling environmental problems at the source, and preferably prevent them from appearing). The *business economics part* includes: (i) Economics, investments, and finance, focusing on cost-benefit analysis, capital requirements calculations, and investment decisions; (ii) Organisation, logistics, and purchasing, focusing on organisational structure, culture, processes, product flows, and the importance of purchasing; and (iii) Marketing and company relations with stakeholders, plus company impacts on stakeholders. Other supporting courses include data processing and methodological writing procedures. The institution cooperates with a regional chemical treatment company on the more technical aspects of the course, i.e. lectures and material on the chemical and biological aspects of the environment and pollution. It has been relatively easy to find material on the technical aspects of the environment. Books and articles on environmental economics and management, especially at the microeconomic level, have been harder to come by, however.

The course is based on lectures. Because of the small number of students, there is much class discussion, although some of the courses (e.g. statistics and economics) are still taught through traditional lectures with examples. The programme includes relatively few traditional examinations, more emphasis being placed on projects about specific problems. The final module of the course consists of a thesis on some relevant problem in the trainee company. The general teaching approach, i.e. based on theory, projects and a trainee period, occupies a rather special place within the country's educational system because of the nature of the trainee period, which is more intensive and planned than "normal" trainee periods. This is also why the trainee period is not called a "practical" period, as is normal in other similar courses. When the contract with the participating companies expires, the institution will have to find new firms. However, some of the companies have indicated that they might continue the cooperation, so the course coordinators are fairly optimistic.

According to the institution, graduates of the course are intended to act as a "glue" or integrator between various functions in companies, e.g. between production and finance, marketing and accounting, production and marketing, etc. They are not expected to suggest specific technical solutions, but to be able to calculate and argue for the consequences of these solutions from an economic, environmental and legal perspective.

Future changes within the institution are expected to include an extension of the theory module preceding the trainee period. Some courses are also expected to be adjusted in line with experience and feedback. Furthermore, there are also plans for expanding into postgraduate education. To that end, a joint project with a local regional authority is currently under way to find new areas and needs for the institution's teaching facilities and expertise.

6.0 CONCLUSIONS AND FUTURE ACTIONS AND ACTIVITIES

6.1 THE PRESENT AND FUTURE ROLE OF INDUSTRIAL LEADERS AND SELF- REGULATION

Environmental self-regulation has often been cited as an (opposite) option to environmental regulation, begging the question as to whether the choice is so clear-cut. This in turn depends on which side of the fence one is sitting - on the political and/or administrative side, or on the business side.

This rather uncompromising either/or dichotomy is far too simplistic to handle such a complex issue as the business-environment relationship. To begin with, efficient environmental regulation, e.g. bans, restrictions, and/or standards, requires a complete knowledge of: optimal ecosystems (and how they function); the exact limit of Nature's carrying capacity; the various multiplier effects caused by the interaction between various polluting substances and effluents; the toxic characteristics of the growing number of new chemicals; and how to establish and operate optimal regulating institutions without any budgetary or HRM constraints (Ulhøi, 1992). None of these requirements can be said to be met today in any of the countries surveyed.

Depending solely on societal institutions to handle environmental problems is not only unsustainable from an ecological point of view (the complexity of ecological systems and their ultimate absorption capacity is still poorly understood), but also from an economic point of view. In countries with a long history of strict environmental regulations, e.g. Germany and Denmark, a hierarchical and bureaucratic system has evolved over the years in which centralised environmental regulators typically oversee local regulators acting in accordance with overall national policy.

The present state of human knowledge is insufficient to fully understand all the complexities of Nature, and is inadequate for separating one type of pollution from another. As a result, it is not clear whether existing standards and limits are sufficient.

This is also why regulation has a tendency to become more and more stringent as the knowledge about the natural ecosystems increases (Ulhøi, 1991). Moreover, the extent to which the regulations are being complied with by industry can never be absolutely ascertained (this would require constant monitoring, which is both economically and practically non-implementable).

Normal corporate economic and general business economic considerations do not favour this strategy either. For example, municipal waste treatment and incineration facilities counteract improvements in environmental performance, both in industry and households, because such systems require a constant inflow of input (waste) in order to operate at a technically and economically acceptable level. As environmental concern in society increases, therefore, and the production of waste decreases, e.g. as a result of the introduction of recycling systems, such centralised waste treatment facilities will find it harder and harder to maintain the inflow, typically forcing them to lower their handling rates in order to increase the supply of waste. Society thus needs to supplement such a command-and-control strategy with other strategies.

Self-regulation (or deregulation) is based on the idea that environmental problems are best dealt with through the market system. Traditionally, however, property rights have never been assigned to environmental "goods", which means that the market mechanism cannot handle environmental problems. Economists have grappled for years with the problem of how property rights can be assigned to environmental "goods" in order to make the market mechanism function. Since the Coasean property right approach was first introduced in 1960, the idea of introducing tradeable permits has emerged as an alternative to the dominant command-and-control paradigm of Western economies. Although this is an interesting aspect, it will not be discussed further here. For an overview, see, for example, Ulhøi (1992).

Self-regulation is based on the fundamental belief that practical solutions to industrial environmental problems are best dealt with by the polluters themselves, since they have both the know-how and the money necessary to solve them. However, abstaining from public environmental regulation and leaving matters entirely in the hands of industry will neither ensure that the general process of change towards a more sustainable development proceeds fast enough nor that it will be efficient enough. Other problems will remain unsolved. First of all, such a strategy does not include the considerable number of environmental problems caused by private households. Second, it will not prevent "free-riders" from cynically exploiting the good will and intentions of concerned corporations. Third, some very harmful wastes, such as radioactive wastes, gene-manipulated/genetically engineered materials, chemicals, etc., need to be strictly accounted for and controlled.

Increasing emphasis on self-regulation can be expected, however, fully in line with both Brundtlandian philosophy and the EU's Fifth Environmental Policy and Action Programme. Nevertheless, national and supranational initiatives will still be necessary in some areas:

- control and regulation of highly toxic materials and substances;

- harmonization of environmental standards for CO_2, NO_x, SO_x, and ozone-depleting gases;

- harmonization of environmental standards in advertising;

- economic incentive schemes to introduce the market mechanism wherever it can work for the benefit of the environment;

- the dissemination of sustainable business practices to the rest of the business community in general and SMEs in particular; and

- the need to address the other pillars of sustainability (the balance between population growth and natural carrying capacity; the balance and equity of the present and future distribution of resources and wealth).

6.2 GENERAL CONCLUSIONS FOR INDUSTRY

This study reflects the state of the art of contemporary environmental and resource management in Europe, based on empirical findings from a selected sample of environmentally leading companies. It thus has no explanatory or generalising power for the rest of the business community in the included countries, only for companies at the "cutting edge" of industrial environmental performance. Unfortunately, these are still a minority.

Based on previous experience and the results of this study, the success of corporate environmental programmes depends not only on the existence of a professional environment manager, but, in particular, on the degree of integration and support at all levels throughout the entire organisation. The study has shown that leading LEs are characterized by: formal structures and managerial procedures to cope with environmental decisions and issues; various kinds of incentives and measurements to sustain and improve environmental performance; various kinds of internal training activities for internal staff, customers, suppliers and other external stakeholders; an emphasis on the need for managers to be trained and educated as generalists; and an emphasis on the need for all key managers and decision-makers to be environmentally literate.

The transformation towards more environmentally sustainable business practices can perhaps best be described as an incremental process of change involving several stages. Some of the implications of this process for industry are illustrated in table 6.1.

Ideally, if the individual company starts from scratch (stage 1), it will typically have to pass through 5 stages before it can properly be called sustainable. The majority of the companies included in this study are somewhere between stages 3 and 4 when compared with the definitions in table 6.1 (probably a little closer to 4 than 3).

Table 6.1. Evolutionary stages of corporate environmental management

Criteria	Stage 1	Stage 2	Stage 3	Stage 4	Stage 5	Stage 6
Environmental protection	No protection	Minimal protection	Moderate protection	Comprehensive protection	Maximum protection	Maximum prevention
Organisational commitment:						
General Mind-set of Corporate Managers	Environmental management is unnecessary	Environmental issues should be addressed only as necessary	Environmental management is a worthwhile function	Environmental management is an important business function	Environmental management is prioritized	Environmental management fully integrated
Resource Commitment	Minimal resource commitment	Budgets for problems as they occur	Consistent, yet minimal budget	Generally sufficient funding	Open-ended funding	Environmental sustainability first priority
Support and involvement of Top Management	No involvement	Piecemeal involvement	Commitment in theory	Aware and moderately involved	Actively involved	As actively involved as every other employee
Programme design:						
Performance objectives	None	Resolve problems as they occur	Satisfy corporate responsibility	Minimize negative environmental impact	Active management of environmental matters	Prevent environmental problems from occuring
Types of performance measures	None	None	Qualitative	Quantitative	Quantitative and qualitative	Sustainability indicators

Criteria	Stage 1	Stage 2	Stage 3	Stage 4	Stage 5	Stage 6
Programme design (*cont.*):						
Integration within the company	Not integrated	Involved with other departments on a piecemeal basis	Minimal interaction with other departments	Moderate integration with other departments	Actively involved with other departments	Fully integrated
Reporting to top management	No reporting	Exceptions, reporting only	Generates voluminous reports that are rarely read	Consistent and targeted reporting	Personal meeting with managers and board of directors	Employees report to all top managers on environmental issues
Reporting structures	None	Exceptions, reporting only	Internal reporting only	Mostly internal, with some external reporting	Internal and external reporting mechanisms	Full public sustainability performance report
Time horizon	Short	Short	Short	Short to medium	Medium	Long
Involvement with:						
- Legal Counsels	None	Moderate	Moderate	High	Daily	Daily
- Public Relations	None	None	Moderate	High	Daily	Daily
- Manufacturing/Production	None	None	None	Moderate	Daily	Daily
- Product Design	None	None	None	Minimal	Daily	Daily
Inclusion of other social issues	None	None	None	None	Some	Extensive

Source: Based on Hunt & Auster (1990)

Another key aspect of the company process towards sustainability is the disclosure of environmental performance to corporate stakeholders. This can also be depicted as a process development, which Deloitte Touche Tohmatsu International et al. (1993) illustrate as reproduced in table 6.1.

Figure 6.1. Evolutionary stages of corporate environmental reporting

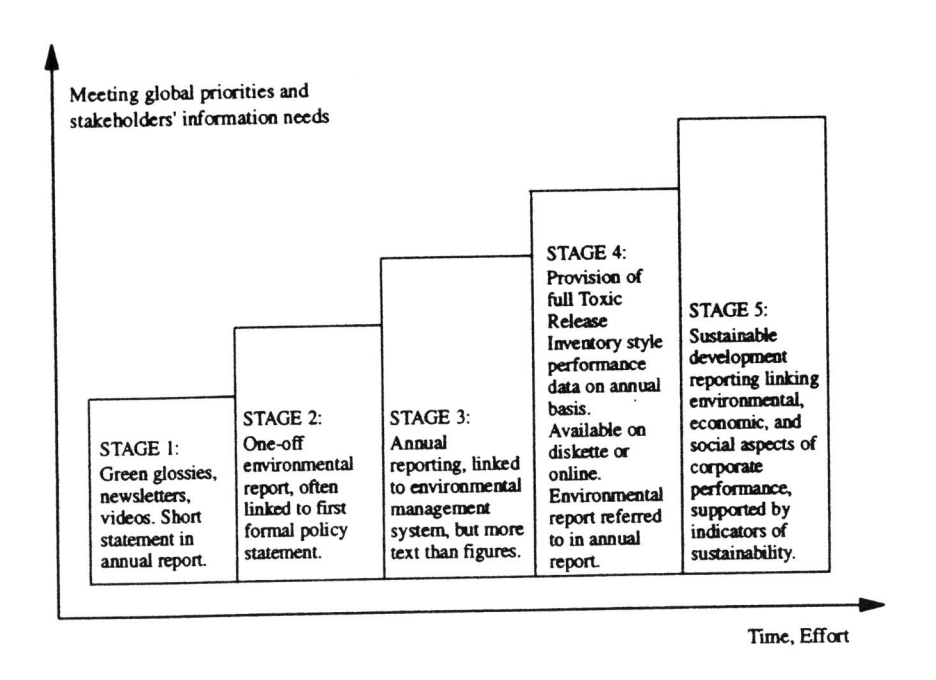

```
Meeting global priorities and
stakeholders' information needs
```

STAGE 1: Green glossies, newsletters, videos. Short statement in annual report.

STAGE 2: One-off environmental report, often linked to first formal policy statement.

STAGE 3: Annual reporting, linked to environmental management system, but more text than figures.

STAGE 4: Provision of full Toxic Release Inventory style performance data on annual basis. Available on diskette or online. Environmental report referred to in annual report.

STAGE 5: Sustainable development reporting linking environmental, economic, and social aspects of corporate performance, supported by indicators of sustainability.

Time, Effort

Source: Deloitte Touche Tohmatsu International et al. (1993, p.10)

In this study, the majority of companies can be grouped in stage 3 when compared with the definitions in figure 6.1. While a couple of companies have begun to move towards stage 4, none is even near stage 5, which includes socio-economic and ethical issues, and where companies must explicitly state how they already have and plan to contribute to a sustainable development.

In other words, industry is still far from being truly sustainable. All the indications so far point to the conclusion that it would be best to continue (for some years) to focus primarily on the environmental dimension before introducing the other pillars of sustainability so as not to frighten the business community unduly. However, this cannot be put off indefinitely, because, as one manager convincingly argued during one of the interviews, these issues are far too important to be left to politicians alone!

A number of areas requiring further organisational development can be deduced from the company findings of the study.

A general shift in primary drivers from cost reduction and legislative compliance to customer demand and corporate image can be observed. Future environment managers must therefore be able to monitor the relevant areas influencing these drivers. The shift from internal economic drivers and external drivers influenced by public opinion (and thus normally known beforehand) to less well-known customer attitudes (a population where differences in opinion will exist) and customer perceptions of a company's image thus requires strategic skills in monitoring market forces. One advantage of doing this is that companies will be able to identify the right time to market new environmental products, thereby avoiding premature launching. A related aspect is that the training of customers in the "correct" environmental use of the product will become more and more standard practice. The training instruments needed will depend on the market, i.e. whether the company operates in the industrial or consumer market, and whether the training is aimed at stakeholders in general.

Another aspect revealed during the study is the conflict between environmental intentions and economic considerations. No standard investment analysis seems to have been carried out on investments brought about by legislation or restrictions as such investments are considered to be non-optional. And there is a lack of appropriate methods, standards and techniques for evaluating and ranking environmental investments made as a result of sincere concern for the environment. Two major reasons for this were identified: (i) the problem of separating environmental costs from other costs, which makes it difficult to measure the effects of an environmental investment, and (ii) the problems of visualising the effects of an environmental investment in a global perspective, which calls for criteria other than traditional ones, such as accepting longer payback periods.

It was noticeable that global aspects are seldom included in evaluations of a company's impact on the environment. One reason for this is the problem of who is to evaluate global influences and relate them to company internal and external (both local and global) economic factors. Another problem is the lack of general quantitative environmental performance indicators for use in monitoring the achievement of environmental goals. Some initial steps have been taken, but much more remains to be done in this area.

Finally, what kind of environment managers will be needed in future? Judging by the present situation, generalists with a specific background in engineering or science might still be acceptable in the near future. In the longer term, however, generalists will mainly be required at corporate level in LEs, with specialists being employed at department levels. This development will increase with the coming of cross-company cooperation in environmental management, which is expected to take place in the future. Such generalists will need a general background in management, including environmental aspects, but will also be able to communicate with technically trained specialists. In any event, future top managers will need sufficient knowledge of environmental consequences, environmental management, etc., to be able to understand the information and signals they receive, both from lower levels in the organisation and external sources.

6.3 THE PRESENT AND FUTURE ROLE OF INSTITUTIONS OF HIGHER EDUCATION

With an expected doubling of the world population and a four- to five-fold increase in economic output projected for the next four to five decades, meeting social needs without transgressing biophysical limits will require no less than a paradigm shift in the way people interact with and exploit the natural environment. Such a radical process of change will involve, and need, the active participation of all social partners, and, in particular, the provision of higher education. This puts institutions of higher education, which produce the key decision-makers of tomorrow (in government and public administration as well as industry), in a strong position. They have - and will continue to have in the future, along with the increasing demand for life-long training and education - an important role to play in the educational, research, and policy developments of society. This gives the social partners a major responsibility to increase the awareness, knowledge, and skills needed to realise an environmentally more sustainable future. Institutions of higher education have long been able to provide highly competent and well-tested frameworks and approaches for handling such complex tasks.

Owing to their influence on future business leaders and policy-makers (through their present students) and existing leaders (through their alumni), institutions of higher education are in a unique position to help society in general, and industry in particular, to adopt more environmentally sustainable paths of development. Before this can happen, however, the institutions need to undergo a period of self-examination in which they make some important changes in both the process (e.g. the existing organisation and career structure, and teaching approaches) and content (i.e. the specialised content) of the courses they offer.

This is also supported by the study, which has found that, while industry's environmental responsibilities and involvement have increased rapidly, the management education system has generally lagged behind. As a result, managers who are today responsible for incorporating environmental concern into business operations and planning are "self-made" and environmentally highly committed individuals, who experience daily conflicts with colleagues lacking any kind of environmental concept in their professional vocabulary.

Institutions of higher education have a responsibility, also emphasised during the interviews, to stay ahead of business in order to provide the business community with the necessary means to cope with problems both before and after they occur. This implies that it is not sufficient just to teach what is practised. On the other hand, it should also be clear that, in order to disseminate the concept of environmental management to as many companies as possible, postgraduate training courses based on existing practices will be required for years to come. Because of national differences in management style and practice (see, for example, Peattie & Ringler, 1994), training activities will almost certainly have different contexts and scope. In order to avoid tedious discussions on the outcome of environmental management, however, it is important that a harmonised approach be adopted as quickly as possible.

Put another way, this study has provided evidence which seriously questions whether the management education system lives up to this important role. The sooner this documented mismatch in the present educational system is corrected, the sooner it will be able to produce graduates better equipped to handle reality as it is and not as it is supposed to be.

6.4 GENERAL CONCLUSIONS FOR EDUCATIONAL INSTITUTIONS

According to Moser and Arnold (1993), business schools and universities have four levels of commitment to curriculum greening. The first level consists of a non-systematic grassroot integration of environmental issues into existing courses in management, accounting, production, finance, etc., and has been found in several of the institutions surveyed in this study. Such an approach suffers from the fact that it does not give the student a broad introduction to environmental issues, however.

At the next level, a single elective course is devoted to environmental management. Although this approach ensures a much broader coverage of the issues (one of the senior members of this research team has been running such a graduate course for years), it invariably only appeals to the "converted", i.e. students who are already interested in environmental issues. This is the dominant approach among the institutions surveyed.

At the third level, the degree programme allows the student to take several courses in the environment and still graduate within a traditional discipline (e.g. business administration). This approach has also been found at a couple of the institutions surveyed.

Finally, some institutions have both faculties of business administration and technical and/or natural sciences, which offer a joint programme. This was found in only one case in this study (a joint PhD programme in Denmark).

This study supports the assertion that we are far from achieving the full integration of environmental concern into higher educational curricula. As already indicated, there may be several reasons for this:

- an insufficient understanding of the interactions between population growth, human activities, and the environment;

- an insufficient understanding of the practical, economic, and social limitations;

- the prevailing organisation into areas of specialised knowledge, and established disciplines fighting to keep and/or increase their "share of the cake";

- the hegemony of the positivistic model of science (PMS) in contemporary natural and social sciences, which, among other things, allows mainstream economics to view the economic system as totally separate from the biophysical system; and

- (as a result of the above) the immanent PMS-led career structure within the academic world, which, among other things, makes it hard to "swim against the tide". As one interviewee, an internationally recognised university academic, stated, "you need to have a couple of well-recognised publications in your belly before you dare (and succeed) to publish a non-mainstream article".

For these reasons, academic institutions are predisposed to turn out traditionally specialised graduates, and, at best in most cases, only offer environmental courses as a voluntary add-on to existing programmes.

The 1990 INSEAD conference report on Environmental Resource Management concluded that there is a need for champions, success models, funding, and curricula materials if a change is ever to take place in institutions of higher education (Moser and Arnold, 1993). This study has shown that, if not for individual champions, the environmental greening process would never have started in educational institutions. As for funding, interviewees have pointed to an alarming lack of financial resources available for sufficiently educated colleagues and educational material. Regarding the latter, the authors of this report are almost daily reminded of this through the various international electronic networks they are hooked into. The first two requirements of the INSEAD report are thus no longer the most critical aims, while the others, e.g. lack of funding and resistance from the scientific (economic) community, have assumed much more importance.

As pointed out by Cortese (1993), there is still a need for a variety of highly educated and trained professionals. Demographers are needed to understand the trends in population growth and to develop strategies to stabilise population levels; scientists are needed to understand the natural world and the efficacy of environmental improvement strategies; health specialists are needed to understand and document the toxic effects of pollution; engineers are needed to develop cleaner technologies; lawyers and policy-makers are needed to develop appropriate environmental regulations; economists and management specialists are needed to evaluate the costs of pollution and to develop preventive managerial strategies; geographers, planners and sociologists are needed to develop solutions to environmental problems that are both socio-economically, socio-politically and socioculturally feasible; and, finally, humanists and philosophers are needed to evaluate the values and motivations (inhibiting as well as catalysing) involved in the implementation of environmentally sustainable developments.

According to UNEP (1993), industry has five major environmental education needs: (i) greater all-round environmental awareness; (ii) environmental education for present and future managers; (iii) training programmes for environmental specialists; (iv) environmental education for engineers and other professionals; and (v) worker education and training. "International co-operation can greatly enhance the reach and effectiveness of environmental education and training for industry, e.g. through the sharing of experience between countries. (...) Industry's environmental education and training needs are immense." (ibid.).

This study reflects the state of the art of contemporary environmental and resource management education in Europe. It has been based on empirical findings from a selected sample of institutions of higher education and other institutions providing environmental management courses of longer duration, and thus has no explanatory or generalising power for other managerial educators in the countries included, only for the those at the "cutting edge" in the EU. Unfortunately, these are still a very small minority.

The inclusion of environmental concern into management curricula can be described as a multi-stage process. The various educational implications of this process are illustrated in table 6.2.

The majority of managerial educators are close to stage 3 when compared with the definitions in table 6.2. This is surprising, since after all, they are expected to be ahead of the development in trade and industry and thus should have been clustered around stage 4 and 5.

The main findings of this study lead, among other things, to a central question: is the development of a harmonised and joint approach to environmental management education and training in the EU feasible, and can financial incentive schemes to encourage this be recommended? Regarding the paradigmatic resistance within the scientific community, it is assumed that this can best be changed by the researchers themselves.

Arguments in favour of such a joint strategy include:

- it has a cost-effective potential;

- it has potential synergetic effects;

- it will lead to faster development and dissemination of the greening process within the educational system;

- individual institutions will not have to "reinvent the wheel" but can concentrate on adaptation and refinement; and

- giving students a "European" education will ease the mobility of human capital.

Arguments against a joint approach include:

- it will have to cope with significant cultural and qualitative differences;

- it may put a brake on innovative new approaches; and

- it will put considerable strain on a few key educators for a period of time, which might force them to neglect their home institutions.

Table 6.2. Evolutionary stages of higher environmental management education

Criteria	Stage 1	Stage 2	Stage 3	Stage 4	Stage 5	Stage 6
Contribution of the educational institution to sustainable development	None	None	Minimum /Moderate	Moderate	Active	Maximum
Institutional commitment:						
General mind-set of educators	Environmental management is ignored	Environmental management is viewed as an add-on	Environmental management is a worthwhile, albeit subordinate discipline	Environmental management is an important teaching discipline	Environmental management is the most important discipline	Environmental management is integrated into all teaching activities
Resource commitment	No resource commitment	Minimal resource commitment	Consistent yet minimal	Moderate funding	Generally sufficient funding	Open-ended funding
Administrative and/or colleague support	No support	Piecemeal involvement	Piecemeal involvement	General commitment	General commitment and active involvement	Full commitment and active involvement
Environmental curricula or courses	None	Few ad hoc	Few ad hoc	Few, but ongoing	Several ongoing	Included in all disciplines

Alternative options:

- new funding (programme) for new and innovative environmental education approaches;

- follow-up research to evaluate and assess the growing number of unconnected experiences among managerial educators; and

- the establishment of an EU database containing environmental management services, for the quick distribution of new teaching materials, curricula, experiences, etc.

The results of the study clearly show that, as regards incorporating environmental issues into existing managerial disciplines and functions, the leading "green" institutions responsible for educating corporate managers lag far behind leading "green" companies. The question is, what can be done to bridge the gap?

This is a very important question, since it bears directly on the raison d'être of management education institutions, which are expected to provide state-of-the-art knowledge and tools for the business community. As such, it is only fair to expect them to be at least a little ahead of the "customers" who are supposed to "buy" their products.

There is no single satisfactory explanation for the state of affairs described in this study. Rather, as the study has amply documented, there are several important factors, which have different weights from one institution to another. Apart from the factors already discussed in this report, it is important to consider how the dialogue between educators and managers can be improved. Several options are frequently suggested: commissioned and sponsored research projects; sponsored chairs and/or departments/centres; corporate representatives in publicly owned educational institutions; mutual exchange of professors and managers; compulsory trainee periods for students in real-life companies during their education. As long as the money and influence of the business community is not directly involved, then most educators will probably have no objections. Opinion is divided on the money issue.

Arguments in favour of a strong corporate relationship to business educators include:

- a higher degree of coherence between expectations and results;

- better funding potentials; and

- shared responsibility for the direction of management education.

Arguments against involvement include:

- a weakening of the scientific autonomy of educational institutions;

- it will be harder to develop new ideas which deviate radically from present knowledge and experience;

- it will be more difficult to criticize company practice.

6.5 FUTURE MANAGERIAL AND EDUCATIONAL NEEDS

Probably one of the loudest messages to managerial educators found in this study is the strongly-felt need for generalists, who, it was argued, are better equipped to understand the complexity and implications of environmental management decisions.

Another very interesting (and, to many, probably surprising) finding of the interviews is that institutions of higher education seem to be among the most advanced users of various teaching approaches and methods, which to some extent reflects a sincere desire to transgress existing disciplinary boundaries.

To further support and speed up this positive development, the following initiatives are suggested:

- funds for new and innovative pilot studies (both national and European), in which different approaches can be tested;

- the development of new "official" degrees (at bachelor, master's and doctoral level) to fill the gap until the environment becomes fully integrated into existing professions;

- the inclusion of senior managers from environmentally leading companies onto the boards of directors of business schools and universities (this has been implemented in Denmark as a result of legislation);

- inclusion of environmental concern as an evaluation performance criterion;

- increasing the amount of commissioned research; and

- co-sponsored chairs for environmental management and economics at business schools. To our knowledge, only five such chairs exist today (in France, Canada, USA, Sweden, and Switzerland).

6.6. FUTURE RESEARCH

It became clear during the TEM-1 project that the relationship between the practice of environmental management and the education of business managers is a topic which has received little attention until now. There is therefore a strong need for more research.

One of the issues raised by TEM-1 focuses on the need for a harmonised and joint approach to environmental management training in the EU.

It soon became apparent that none of the corporate managers included in this study had any precise knowledge of the managerial requirements for their jobs. Such knowledge tends to be largely tacit knowledge. Environment managers know what to do, but they have given less thought to how they do it. Furthermore, none of the educational institutions offering environmental courses had systematically surveyed and evaluated industry's requirements.

Thus an obvious issue for future research is: "What are the more specific and detailed environmental management education and training requirements of industry?" Any attempt to provide a definitive answer to this question would require examining the actual environmental tasks performed by management, the demands of external influences such as legislation, and identifying which decision-makers actually influence environmental decisions, etc. Such knowledge can only be obtained by means of a different research design, for example through a closer collaboration with environmental and corporate managers over a period of time.

A second, related research issue would be to provide a more detailed picture of lower management and employee environmental education and training requirements, in cooperation with organisations such as CEDEFOP, the Task Force on Human Resources, ILO, OECD, and national branch/industry organisations. The aim here is to determine how the greening of business can be further supported and advanced.

Attention also needs to be directed towards the corporate board level and present types of ownership, and to investigate the extent to which corporate board members, and their values and beliefs, influence the scope and depth of strategic greening actions taken by CEOs and top management.

More research needs to be done on how environmental management systems and environmental knowledge and technology can be transferred from LEs to SMEs. Although this issue has already been much discussed within the areas of strategic management and the transfer of knowledge and technology, the environmental management dimension seems to be lacking.

There is also a need to explore how environmental management systems can be further developed, particularly as regards strategic monitoring of environmental variables and developing quantitative indicators of environmental performance.

A major research need in the area of corporate finance and accounting is how to define environmental costs and separate them from other costs. This requires an investigation of both direct and indirect environmental costs, and the development of a comparable standard for companies and industries.

Finally, there is a need to examine and redefine the core values, beliefs, assumptions and motives of companies regarding environmental issues. Most corporate decisions are influenced by the beliefs and values of both management and employees, but the final decision is also the result of various assumptions and motives of different corporate actors. How, for example, global/societal aspects can be introduced into company decision-making is an important issue for future research.

ANNEX 1

LIST OF REFERENCES

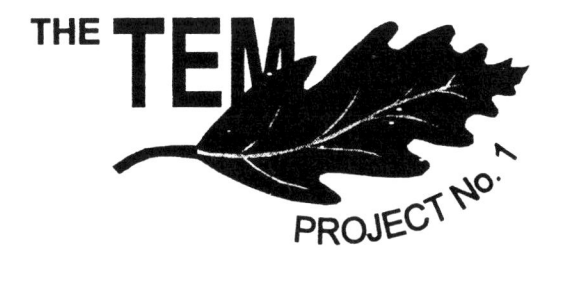

Bennet, S. J. (1991). *Ecopreneuring*. N. Y.: John Wiley & Sons, Inc.

Braat, L. C. & Steetskamp, I. (1994). Ecological-Economic Analysis for Regional Sustainable Development. In: Constanze, R. (ed.). *Ecological Economics: The Science and Management of Sustainability*. N.Y. Columbia University Press.

Business International (1990). *Managing the Environment: The Greening of European Business*. London: Business International, Ltd.

Catton Jr., W. R. (1987). The World's Most Polymorphic Species: Carrying Capacity Transgressed Two Ways. *BioScience*, **37**(6), 413-419.

COM (1992a) 23/III. *"Miljøsituationen i det Europæiske Fællesskab"*, Catalogue number CB-CO-92-151-DA-C, Kommissionen for de Europæiske Fælleskaber, Office for the Official Publications of the European Communities, Luxembourg.

COM (1992b). Proposal for a Resolution of the Council of the European Communities on a Community Programme of Policy and Action in Relation to the Environment and Sustainable Development, 23 Final 27/3/92.

COM (1992c). Communication of the Commission to the Council and to the European Parliament: Industrial Competitiveness and Protection of the Environment. SEC/92/1986 Final.

Constanza, R. (1989). What is Ecological Economics. *Ecological Economics*, **1**, 1-7.

Cortese, A. D. (1993). Building the Intellectual Capacity for a Sustainable Future. *Industry and Environment*, **16**(4), 6-10.

Daly, H. E. (ed.) (1980). *Economics, Ecology, Ethics. Essays Towards A Steady-State Economy*. San Francisco: W.H.Freeman and Company.

Deloitte Touche Tohmatsu Int., International Institute for Sustainable Development & SustainAbility (1993). *Coming Clean-Corporate Environmental Reporting: Opening up for Sustainable Development*. London: Deloitte Touche Tohmatsu.

Ecotec (1992). *Education and Training of Personnel Concerned With Environmental Issues Relating to Industry*. Dublin: European Foundation for the Improvement of Living and Working Conditions.

Eurostat (1991). *"Environmental Statistics"*, Office for the Official Publications of the European Communities, Luxembourg.

Gladwin, T. N. & Welles, J. G. (1976). Environmental Policy and Multinational Corporate Strategy. In: Walter, I. (ed.). *Studies in International Environmental Economics.* N.Y.: John Wiley & Sons.

Goodland, R. (1992). The Case That the World has reached Limits: More Precisely That Current Throughput Growth in Global Economy Cannot Be Sustained. In: Goodland, R., Daly, H., Serafy, S. E. & Droste, B. v. (eds.). *Environmentally Sustainable Development: Building on Brundtland.* Paris: UNESCO.

Goodland, R. & Ledec, G. (1987). Neoclassical Economics and Sustainable Development. *Ecological Modelling*, **38**, 19-46.

Goodland, R., Daly, H., Serafy, S. E. & Droste, B. v. (eds.) (1992). *Environmentally Sustainable Development: Building on Brundtland.* Paris: UNESCO.

Hardin, G. (1991). Paramount Positions in Ecological Economics. In *Ecological Economics: The Science and Management of Sustainability.* N.Y.: Columbia University Press.

Heaton, G., Repetto, R. & Sobin, S. (1991). *Transforming Technology: An Agenda for Environmental Sustainable Growth in the 21st Century.* Washington D.C.: World Resource Institute.

Hueting, R. (1990). The Brundtland Report: A Matter of Conflicting Goals. *Ecological Economics*, **2**, 109-117.

Hunt, C. B. & Auster, E. R. (1990). Proactive Environmental Management: Avoiding the Toxic Trap. *Sloan Management Review*, **21**, 7-18.

International Chamber of Commerce (1991). *ICC Guide to Effective Environmental Auditing.* ICC Publication No. 483. ICC Publishing.

International Chamber of Commerce (1992). Position Paper on Environmental Education. Document no. 210/414.

International Labour Office (1992). ILO Activities for Environment and the World of Work. Geneva: International Labour Office.

Karshenas, M. (1992). Environmental Development and Employment: Some

Conceptual Issues. In: Bhalla, A. S. (ed.). *Environment, Employment and Development*. Geneva: International Labour Office.

KPMG International (1993). International Survey of Environmental Reporting. KPMG International.

Madsen, H., Rikhardsson P. M. & Ulhøi J. P. (1993). *Sustainable Corporate Management in Denmark: Preliminary Results from a Survey of the Present Greening Situation in Danish Industry*. Denmark, DEMS Working Paper No. 2, Department of Information Science, The Aarhus School of Business.

Milbrath, L.W. (1989). *Envisioning a Sustainable Society*. Albany: State University of New York Press.

Moser, M. & Arnold, M. (1993). The Greening of Business Schools. *Industry and Environment*, 16(4), 17-21.

Norgaard, R. (1988). Sustainable Development: A Co-Evolutionary View, *Futures*, 20(6), 606-620.

North, K. (1992). *Environmental Business Management. An Introduction*. Geneva: International Labour Office.

Nulty, P. (1990). Recycling has become big business. *Fortune*, 122(Aug. 13), 81-86.

O'Riordan, T. (1988). The Politics of Sustainability. In: Turner, R. K. (ed.). *Sustainable Environmental Development. Principles and Practice*. London: Belhaven Press.

OECD (1991a). *"Environmental Indicators - A Preliminary Set"*. Paris: OECD Publications Bureau.

OECD (1991b). *"The State of the Environment"*. Paris: OECD Publications Bureau.

OECD (1992). *The OECD environment industry: situation, prospects and government policies*. Paris: OECD Publications Bureau.

Pearce, D. W. (1988). Sustainable Development. *Futures*, 20, 595-678.

Pearce, D. W. & Markandya, A. (1989). Marginal Opportunity Cost as a Planning Concept in Natural Resource Planning. In: Schramm, G. & Warford, J.J. (eds.). *Environmental Management and Economic Development*. Baltimore: John Hopkins University Press.

Peattie, K. & Ringler, A. (1994). Management and the Environment in the UK and Germany: A Comparison. *European Management Journal*, **12**, 216-225.

Peters, T. (1990). *Lean, green and clean: the profitable company of the year 2000*. Presentation to "The greening of European business Conference", held on 4-5 October, 1990, in Munich.

Porter, M. E. (1990). *The competitive advantage of nations*. London: The MacMillan Press, Ltd.

Redclift, M. (1987). *Sustainable Development: Exploring the Contradictions*. London: Methuen.

Repetto, R. (ed.) (1985). *The Global Possible. Resources, Development, and the New Century*. New Haven: Yale University Press.

Rikhardsson, P. M., Ulhøi J. P. & Madsen H. (1993). *Sustainable Corporate Management in Denmark: Research Agenda and Planning the Initial Interview Survey*. Denmark, DEMS Working Paper No. 1, Department of Information Science, The Aarhus School of Business.

Roome, N. (1992). *"Management and Environment"*. Report from a survey conducted for the Manchester Business School, personal correspondance.

Rubenstein, D. B. (1990). *Bridging the gap between green accounting and black ink*. Paper presented at the "EIASM workshop on accounting for new financial instruments at the London School of Economics", December 10-12, 1990.

Schmidheiny, S. (1992). *Changing Course. A Global business Perspective on Development and the Environment*. Cambridge, MA: The MIT Press.

Serafy, S. E. (1992). Sustainability, Income Measurement and Growth. In: Goodland, R., Daly, H., Serafy, S. E. & Droste, B. v. (eds.). *Environmentally Sustainable Development: Building on Brundtland*. Paris: UNESCO.

Stead, W. E. & Stead, J. G. (1992). *Management for a Small Planet - Strategic Decision making and the Environment*. London: Sage.

Tolba, M. K. (1982). *Development Without Destruction: Evolving Environmental Perceptions*. Dublin: Tycooly Publishing Ltd.

Turner, R. K. (ed.) (1988). *Sustainable Environmental Development. Principles and Practice*. London: Belhaven Press.

Ulhøi, J. P. (1991). Virksomheden og det Ydre Miljø, *Virksomhedens Strategi og Ledelse*, **7/91**, 7-23.

Ulhøi, J. P. (1992). *Corporate Greening. The Global Trend of the Next Millenium*. In Proceedings of the International Engineering Management Conference '92, October 1992, New Jersey.

Ulhøi, J. P. (1993). Greening of Industry. Strategic Challenges and Corporate Responses. In: B.S. Kang & J. U. Choi (eds.). *Managing in the Global Economy. A Decision Sciences Perspective*. Seoul: Sungrim Press.

Ulhøi, J. P. (1994). *Corporate Environmental and Resource Management. In Search of a New Managerial Paradigm*. Invited Review in The Journal of Operational Research. Forthcoming.

UNEP (1993). Education for Sustainable Industry (editorial). *Industry and Environment,* **16**(4), 3.

Vellinga, P. (1993). *"Trends in Environmental Education"*. Workshop held in Zandwoort, Holland, March 23-24, 1993.

WCED (World Commission on Environment and Development) (1987). *Our Common Future*. Oxford: Oxford University Press.

Welford, R. & Gouldson, A. (1994). *Environmental Management & Business Strategy*. London: Pitman Publishing.

ANNEX 2

THE GENERAL STATUS OF THE EUROPEAN ENVIRONMENT

THE TEM PROJECT No. 1

A.2 THE GENERAL STATUS OF THE EUROPEAN ENVIRONMENT

The environment is not static, but is constantly changing due to the effects of natural and human activities. In Brundtlandian terms, the change can be said to be negative if it jeopardizes or lessens the chances of future generations to enjoy the same environmental quality as the present generation - i.e. purity of air and water supplies, protection from the harmful rays of the sun, regulation of temperature, access to the same biological diversity, absence of carcinogenic substances in food, etc.

In the above sense, therefore, the state of the environment in the European Union can be said to be deteriorating. Although the EU covers a large area and includes a range of different environmental conditions, and while some improvements have certainly been made, the number of areas and issues where the situation has changed for the worse is greater than where the situation has improved. The following looks at air quality, water quality, soil quality, wastes, biological diversity, public opinion towards environmental issues, the costs of environmental pollution, and the level of environmental expenditure in the EU. The discussion is on a general descriptive level, accompanied by examples from (mainly) France, Germany, Britain and Denmark, which are included in the study. The aim is to give a general introduction to the state of the environment in the European Union and show the basic rationale for the focus on human environmental relations.

This section is based primarily on Commission statistics on the state of the environment in the European Union (COM, 1992a), together with the latest Eurostat Environmental Statistics (Eurostat, 1991). In general, European environmental statistics suffer from a lack of consistency and measurement uniformity, and much of the information is relatively old. Therefore, only information which is recent, uniformly measured, and reported for all 12 Member States is included in the following.

A.2.1 Air quality

Environmental problems related to air pollution include human health impacts, water acidification, the impact on natural ecosystems, depletion of the ozone layer, the greenhouse effect, and destruction of the architectural heritage.

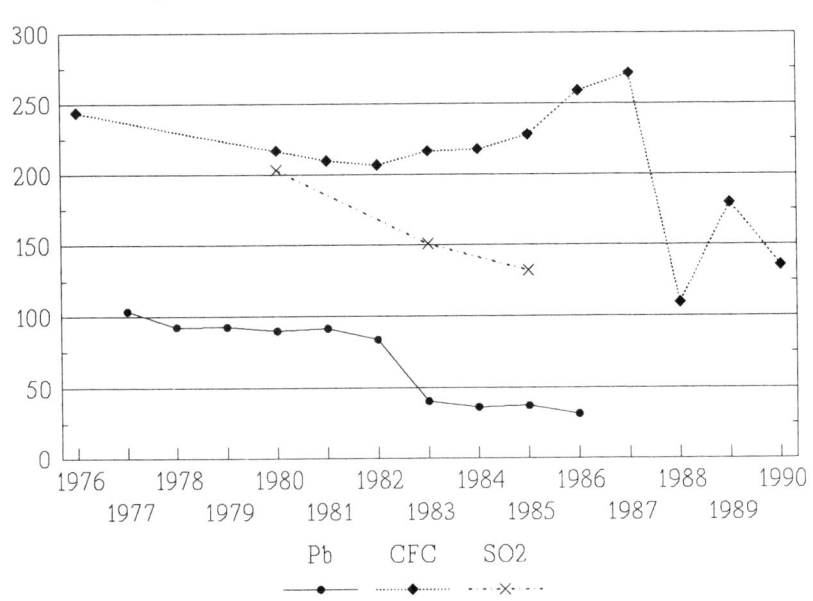

Figure A.1. Pb & SO₂ emissions and CFC consumption

Notes: (i) Emission of Pb from petrol-driven vehicles in 100 t (DK, IRL, NL, UK); (ii) Emission of SO$_2$ in 100,000 t (EU excl. GR); (iii) Sold quantity of CFC in 1000 t (76-80 EU9, 81-85 EU10, 86-90 EU12).
Source: Eurostat (1991)

Some improvement has been made in the European Union as a whole, viz. reductions in SO$_2$, lead, CFC, and particle emissions. This is shown for selected countries in figure A.1. But the problems are still immense and new ones are continually appearing, e.g. depletion of the ozone layer. The EU has outlined a scenario for the year 2000 which includes current and planned initiatives, laws, regulations, and increases in the European car fleet. This predicts a decrease in VOC, CO, and NO$_x$ emissions, and a considerable reduction of SO_2, beginning in 1995 and subsequently stabilising. European emissions of CO_2, however, currently at 12.9% of the world total, are expected to increase. Though the figures show a reduction in total emissions, the situation is expected to deteriorate in areas where urban and industrial growth is allowed to proceed unregulated. Thus, a general improvement of air quality in the EU is not to be expected.

Germany is the second largest European producer of SO_2 and NO_x, although SO_2 emissions per capita place it (and France) among the five lowest. The United Kingdom and Denmark, on the other hand, take the lead in SO_2 emissions per capita. In the UK, 75% of SO_2 emissions are caused by industrial combustion, the same as in Spain and Greece. The UK has the highest total production of SO_2 per capita in the whole of the EU, the third highest production of NO_x, and the second highest production of VOCs.

A.2.2 Water quality

In spite of large investments over the past twenty years, there are more regions where the situation has worsened than where it has improved. Considering the growing demand for water, many regions (e.g. around the Mediterranean) are likely to exhaust their water resources in the near future unless something is done soon to regulate water use.

The main problem, however, is the pollution of aquifers, which affects the quality of ground water. In many regions, the use of ground water as drinking water is problematic, or will become so in the near future. Many coastal regions and deltas experience eutrophication and pollution, and there are no major improvements in sight. Water acidification is increasing, and many pollutants which have not been measured in the past will soon begin to show their effects, e.g. various types of pesticides and herbicides.

On the other hand, the water quality of German rivers has generally improved (see figure A.2) since 1975, although some parts of the Saar, Rhine, Main and Emscher are still classified as "very polluted". The reduction of some environmental impacts in the Rhine is shown in figure A.2.

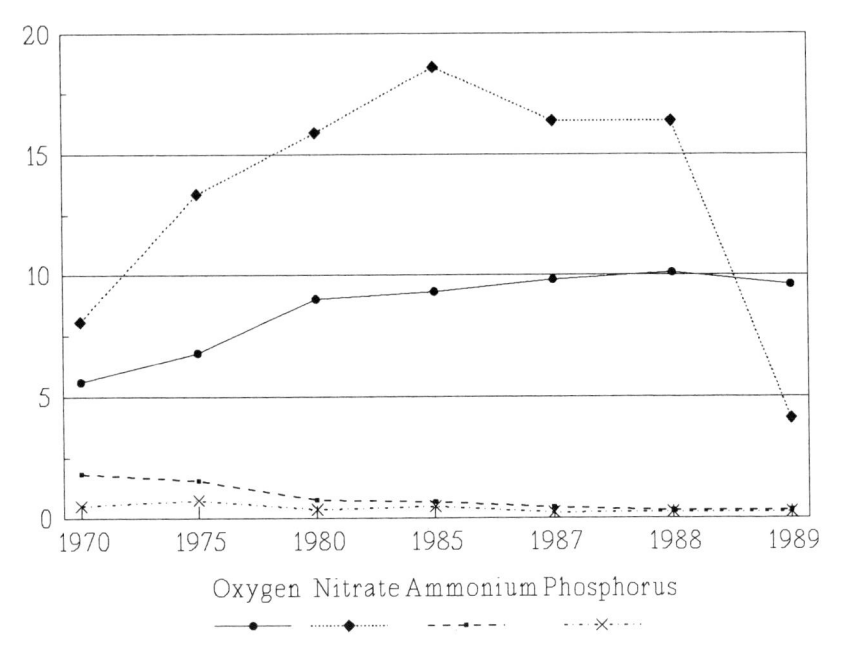

Figure A.2. Water quality in the Rhine

Oxygen Nitrate Ammonium Phosphorus

Note: (i) dissolved mg O_2 per l; (ii) mg NO_3 per l; (iii) mg NH_4 per l; (iv) mg P per l.
Source: Eurostat (1991)

In the UK, 68% of drinking water comes from surface water, and water use is mainly registered as use by the general public and "other" users. The average quality of surface water in the UK has remained stable over the past few years, but eutrophication has caused serious local problems in rivers, dams, estuaries and bays. Some areas suffer from a high nitrate content in the ground water. In France, water is used mainly for cooling purposes and by the general public. Serious local problems have been identified regarding the eutrophication of natural lakes, estuaries and bays. Herbicide and pesticide residues in ground water have increased 50-100% since 1975, and there has been a general deterioration in the quality of bathing water. In Denmark, 99% of drinking water comes from ground water. There are serious problems on a national scale regarding the eutrophication of estuaries and bays, and local problems with coastal water. The average nitrate content of drinking water has doubled three times over the last 30 years. Increases in the use of herbicides and pesticides also affect water quality.

A.2.3 Soil quality

Rural and urban land throughout the EU has suffered extensive damage, threatening such vital functions as the production of agricultural and forest biomass, living environments and regulative functions. The amount of polluting substances measured in the soil has risen in many areas. While heavy metal and organic pollution is serious in urban and industrial areas, agricultural areas have also deteriorated due to air pollution and the effects of over-fertilizing, pesticides, etc. Erosion is still a great problem, especially in the south. Soil deterioration is expected to continue well into the next century, both because environmentally sound agricultural techniques are slow to diffuse and because the cleaning up of numerous waste deposits and polluted industrial sites takes a long time and as yet receives low priority.

The acidification of soil and water in Germany was first identified as a problem in the 1970s, and Germany now participates in an EU observation network to gather information about this environmental issue. Erosion problems plague the south of France, where 49% of the total area in the region is currently classified as a high-risk area. Other soil-related environmental problems include deposits of heavy metals from industrial activities. Heavy metal levels can be 20-30 times as high in industrial areas than in normal populated areas. Heavy metal pollution makes over 40% of the soil in central London and 20% of the soil in urban areas unsuitable for growing vegetables.

A.2.4 Waste

The quantity of waste produced in the European Union is growing faster than the capacity of treatment and removal facilities. Municipal waste, in spite of efforts to increase recycling and composting, is still mainly disposed of in rubbish tips. The development in municipal waste for the four countries in the survey (see section 1.7) is shown in figure A.3.

Figure A.3. Municipal waste (1000 t)

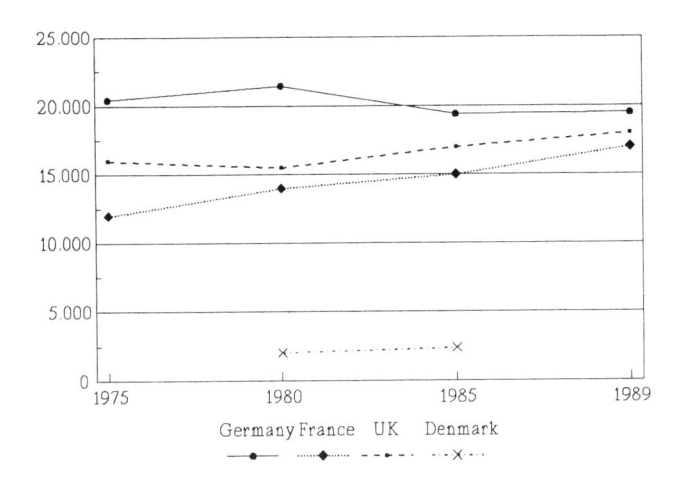

Source: Eurostat (1991)

The quantity of industrial waste is increasing in areas of industrial growth, and the generation of industrial waste far outpaces waste treatment plants, particularly for hazardous wastes. Today, there are tens of thousands of areas polluted by industrial and municipal wastes in the EU.

With an estimated 35,000 potentially polluted sites, Germany is the largest producer of toxic and hazardous waste in the Community. Most of Germany's regular waste is deposited in landfills, while in France it is partly incinerated (36%), incinerated with energy recovery (23%), or used as landfill (47%). Nearly all waste produced in the UK is deposited in landfills, and, with around 1200 sites, the country has the largest number of landfills in the EU. The UK is the second largest producer of toxic and hazardous waste in the Community. In Denmark, waste is mostly either incinerated or used as landfill.

A.2.5 Biological diversity

Generally speaking, biological diversity in the EU is declining. Many animal species, which require large amounts of space for survival, are endangered, and the same goes for many forested areas. There are fewer large water-based ecosystems, and those which are left are in danger of disappearing, thus further reducing the biological diversity.

A major problem in evaluating the reduction in biological diversity is the lack of consistent information. While there have been many individual studies and investigations, most of them have been sporadic and unconnected. Nevertheless, the trend is unmistakable - a decline in many of the ecosystems which support a major part of the biological diversity in the EU, i.e. moorland, bogs, river deltas and forests around the Mediterranean.

A.2.6 Public opinion in the EU towards the environment

The European Commission carried out surveys of public opinion towards the environment and environmental problems in 1987, 1989, and 1991. Of those who were asked in 1991, 88% considered environmental protection to be a very important problem. The UK came in top place, with 91% of the population who considered environmental problems to be of prime importance, followed by Denmark, Germany and Luxembourg (90%), while Portugal (81%), Belgium (83%) and France (85%) came in bottom. Problems such as Third World aid, unemployment, and poverty were considered less important. A majority of the people asked about the causes of the greenhouse effect, acid rain and ozone depletion gave inefficient energy technologies, chemical products, solid fuels and oil, and the destruction of forests as the main causes of these problems. It was evident that citizens of all Member States preferred environment-related decisions to be taken by the EU rather than by their own governments. More than 70% of those questioned expected that the EU would soon adopt common laws for the protection of the environment. Surveys in the USA and Japan have shown that there is a general willingness to give protection of the environment priority over economic growth (71% of those asked in USA and 36% in Japan).

A.2.7   Economic aspects of environmental pollution

Measuring the cost of environmental pollution in the EU is relatively straightforward if it has acquired value through the market mechanism. If not, then costs can be measured by indirect methods and measurements, although these methods have a number of shortcomings and have been widely criticized for being methodologically weak and inconclusive. However, they can give an indication of the extent of the damage, particularly when connected to traditional economic indicators such as GDP, GNP, and national budgets.

Damage caused by total air pollution was estimated to be 0.18% of GDP in The Netherlands and 0.18% in the UK. The damage caused by air pollution due to transport was estimated at 0.4% of GDP in France, 0.15-0.20% in The Netherlands, and 0.4% in Germany in 1984. An estimated DEM 211 billion is needed to repair environmental damage in the former GDR until the year 2000. This includes money for cleaning contaminated industrial sites, installing sewage systems, and upgrading and extending waste water treatment capacity for municipal and industrial facilities.

Information about the costs of environmental damage is not systematically collected in the EU, and different methods have been used to calculate the above figures, which makes them somewhat less useful.

A.2.8 Environmental expenditure

Environmental expenditure is defined as the costs and investments required to prevent, repair, or protect against environmental damage, implement environmental policy, and check the performance of environmental authorities and facilities. The aim of these expenditures is to secure and improve the services and qualities associated with a healthy environment. Germany and Holland lead the EU in environmental expenditures as a percentage of GDP, 1.6% and 1.4% respectively. At the other end are Spain with 0.6% and Ireland and Portugal with 0.8%.

Environmental investments in business are difficult to compare, mainly because of different accounting standards in the member countries and different definitions of environmental investments and cleaner technology. However, comparing investments classified as environmental investments as a percentage of total business investments puts Germany in the lead with 7.7%, followed by The Netherlands with 3.4%, and France with 2.9%. Portugal with 0.1%, Spain with 0.2%, and Italy with 0.3% lag far behind.

A.2.9 Summary

An index has been calculated to summarize environmental impacts and their relative importance in the various EU Member States (see table A.1). The percentage index measures the relative impact of pollution of the production and consumption structure of the country, e.g. the relative share of chemical production in the Community, proportion of fossil fuel consumption, etc. The higher the figure, the greater the impact. Apart from the indices, total population (in millions), population density per square kilometre, and GDP per capita (in ECUs) are also given for comparison. The numbers in brackets in the last column denote the percentage of GNP devoted to environmental expenditure in the statistical material.

As measured by the above index, the larger countries, with higher GDP per capita, heavier industry, and higher population density, have a greater impact on the environment than the other countries. This group includes Germany, France, the UK and Italy. However, the countries with the highest environmental expenditures as a percentage of GNP are Germany, Denmark, The Netherlands and the UK. The actual pressure on the environment is thus not necessarily commensurate with the perceived need to invest in environmental protection.

There is no doubt that progress has been made in some areas regarding environmental protection. As yet, however, environmental measures have not been unduly expensive, ranging from 0.6% to 1.6% of GNP, which means that increases will probably be necessary in the future. In general, the trend revealed by the EU statistics mirrors that in OECD statistics, which reach the same conclusions as regards the state of the environment in OECD Europe and OECD World (OECD 1991a; 1991b).

Table A.1. Index of environmental impact in the EU member states and various characteristics

Country	Index	Population (mill)	Population density/km²	GDP pr. cap. (ECU)
Belgium	4.5	9.9	326	11,965 (-)
Denmark	1.7	5.1	119	15,576 (1,1)
Germany	22.9	62.1	250	14,754 (1.6)
Greece	2.5	10	76	4,701 (-)
Spain	9.8	38.8	77	6,721 (0.6)
France	16.0	56.2	102	13,807 (1.0)
Ireland	1.1	3.5	50	8,049 (1.0)
Italy	17.1	57.5	191	11,074 (0.8)
Luxembourg	-	0.4	146	14,641 (-)
The Netherlands *	5.2	14.8	358	12,314 (1.4)
Portugal	2.0	9.9	107	3,287 (0.8)
UK	17.2	57.2	234	12,250 (1.2)
EU(12)	**(11) 100**	**325.5**	**144**	**11,633**

Sources: COM (1992a); Eurostat (1991)

ANNEX 3

PHASE 1 CONTACTS

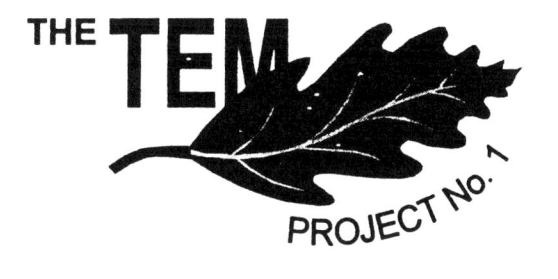

The Association of European
Universities
CRE
Dr. Peri Pamir
10 Conseil-Général
CH-1211 Genève 4
Switzerland

British Standards Institution
Environment Office
Mr. Chris Sheldon
Linford Wood
Milton Keynes MK14 6LE
U.K.

Business Council for Sustainable
Development
Mr. Stephen Schmidheiny
Mr. F. W. Bosshardt
World Trade Centre
3rd floor
10 route l'Aéroport
CH-1215 Geneva 15
Switzerland

Bundesverband der Deutschen
Industrien
Dr. Racke
Mr. Dittmann
Department of Environmental
Policy
Gustaf Heinemann Ufer 84-88
Postfach 510548
D-5000 Köln 51 (Bayenthal)
Germany

C3E
Université de Paris I -
Panthéon Sorbonne
Professor Sylvie Faucheux
Centre National de la Recherche
Scientifique
U.R.A. No. 919
Centre Pierre Mendès France
90 Rue de Tolbiac
F-75013 Paris
France

Centrum voor Beleid &
Management
Universiteit van Utrecht
Dr. C. G. Le Blansch
Muntstraat 2A
3512 EV Utrecht
The Netherlands

Confederation of British Industry
Environment Management Unit
Ms. Karen Howells
Centre Point
103 New Oxford Street
London WC1A 1DU
U.K.

Department of Trade and Industry
Environment Division
Ms. Lyn Bishun
151 Buckingham Palace Road
London SW1W 9SS
U.K.

Ecological Management Foundation
Dr. Allerd Stikker
Prinsengracht 840
1017 JM Amsterdam
The Netherlands

European Trade Union
Confederation
Mr. Michel Miller
Blvd. Emile Jacqmain 155
1210 Brussels
Belgium

European Roundtable of
Industrialists
Secretariat Office
Rue Guimard 15
1040 Brussels
Belgium

Fédération Europénne des
Moyennes et des Grandes
Enterprises
Mr Bernard Le Marchand
Avenue Victor Gilsoul 76
1200 Brussels
Belgium

Henley Management College
Dr. Suzanne Pollack
Greenlands, Henley-on-Thames
Oxfordshire RG9 3AU
U.K.

INSEAD
Professor H. Landis Gabel
Professor Robert Ayres
Boulevard de Constance
F-77305 Fontainebleau Cedex
France

Institut für Europaische
Umweltpolitik e.V.
Ms. Anja Köhne
Roonstrasse 7
D-53175 Bonn
Germany

Institut für Ökologie und
Unternehmungsführung e.V.
European Business School
Dr. Ulrich Steger
Burgstrasse 4
D-653875 Oestrich-Winkel
Germany

Institut für Ökologische
Wirtschaftsforschung
Mr. Jens Clausen
Bergheimer Strasse 97
D-69115 Heidelberg
Germany

Institut für Ökologische
Wirtschaftsforschung
Mr. Klaus Fichter
Giesenbrechtstrasse 13
D-10629 Berlin
Germany

The Institute of Management
Ms. Trudy Coe
3rd Floor
2 Savoy Court
Strand
London WC2R 0EZ
U.K.

International Chamber of
Commerce
Commission of Environment
Mrs. Denise O'Brian
38 Cour Albert 1er
F-75008 Paris
France

Katholieke Universiteit Nijmegen
Faculteit der Natuurwetenschappen
Vakgroep Milieukunde
Dr. D. J. W. Schoof
Postbus 9010
6500 GL Nijmegen
The Netherlands

London Business School
Faculty of Economics
Associate Professor Scott Barrett
Sussex Place
Regent's Park
London NW1 4SA
U.K.

Leeds Metropolitan University
School of the Environment
Professor Peter Roberts
Brunswick Building
Brunswick Terrace
Leeds LS2 8BU
U.K.

National Association for
Environmental Education
General Secretary Brian Milton
University of Wolverhampton
Walsall Campus
Gorway
Walsall WS1 3BD
U.K.

Oxford Brooks University
School of Planning
Professor Elizabeth Wilson
Gipsy Lane Campus
Headington, Oxford OX2 OX2 0BP
U.K.

The Open University
Business Development &
Marketing Office
Mr. Mark Yoxon
Walton Hall
Milton Keynes
MK7 6AA
U.K.

Politecnico de Milano
Dipartimento di Economia e
Produzione
Dr. Giovanni Azzone
Piazza Leonardo da Vinci 32
20133 Milano
Italy

Schweizerische Vereinigung für
Ökologisch bewusste
Unternehmungsführung
Mr. Arthur Braunschweig
Im Stieg 7
CH-8134 Adliswil
Switzerland

UNEP
Industry and Environment Activity
Centre
Mr. John Kryger
Tour Mirabeau
39-43 Quai André Citroen
F-75739 Paris Cedex 15
France

University of East Anglia
Centre for Social and Economic
Research on the Global
Environment
CSERGE
Executive Director R. Kerry
Turner
Norwich
Norfolk NR4 7TJ
U.K.

University of Edinburgh
Department of Accounting and
Business Method
Professor George Harte
William Robertson Building
50 George Square
Edinburgh EH8 9JY
Scotland

University of Huddersfield
School of Accountancy, Law &
Management
Professor David Owen
Queensgate
Huddersfield HD1 3DH
U.K.

University of London
Wye College
ESRC Research Programme
Professor Michael Redclift
Mr. Allister Scott
Wye
Kent TN25 5AH
U.K.

University of Oldenburg
Institut für Politikwissenschaft II -
Politik und Gesellschaft
Prof. Dr. Eberhard Schmidt
Postfach 2503
D-2900 Oldenburg
Germany

University of Plymouth
Plymouth Business School
Professor Andrew Hutchinson
Drake Circus
Plymouth
Devon PL4 8AA
U.K

University of Warwick
Warwick Business School
Dr. Gordon Murray
Coventry CV4 7AL
U.K.

ANNEX 4

PHASE 2 CONTACTS

Companies and educational institutions marked with an "*" were also interviewed

Aalborg University*
Department of Development and
Planning
Professor Arne Remmen
Research Fellow Eskild Holm
Nielsen
Fibigerstraede 2
DK-9220 Aalborg
Denmark

The Aarhus School of Business
Dr. John Parm Ulhøi
Department of Organisation and
Management
Haslegaardsvej 10
DK-8210 Aarhus V
Denmark

B&Q plc
Environmental Department
Dr. Allan P. Knight
Environmental Policy Controller
Portswood House
1 Hampshire Corporate Park
Chandlers Ford
Eastleigh
Hants SO5 3YX
U.K.

Baer Weichkäserei AG
Mr. Stephan Baer
General Manager
Bahnhofstrasse
CH-6403 Küssnacht-am-Rigi
Switzerland

BASF AG
Umwelt, Arbeitssicherheit und
Energie
Zentrale Aufgaben
Dr. Malle
D-67056 Ludwigshafen
Germany

Bayer AG
WV Umweltschutz
Prof. Dr. H. Hulpke
Dr. B. Sewkow
Bayerwerk
D-51368 Leverkusen
Germany

Bischof und Klein GmbH & Co
Umweltschutz
Mr. Kolar
Mr. Bierbaum
Postfach 11
D-49511 Lengerich
Germany

Body Shop International plc
Dr. David Wheeler
General Manager - Environment
Health and Safety
Watersmead
Littlehampton
West Sussex BN17 6LS
U.K.

Boots The Chemist*
Merchandise Technical Services
The Environmental Department
Ms. Belinda K. Howell
Environmental Project Manager
Nottingham NG2 3AA
U.K.

Braas GmbH
Umweltschutz
Ms. Dorothee Kächele
Frankfurter Landstrasse 2-4
D-61437 Oberursel
Germany

British Airways*
Environment Branch
Dr. Hugh Somerville
Mr. Gary Meades
Speedbird House (5285)
PO Box 10
Heathrow Airport
Hounslow
Middlesex TW6 2JA
U.K.

British Gas plc
Dr. M. J. Arnold
Director of Safety and Environment
Safety and Environment Directorate
100 Rochester Row
London SW1P 1JP
U.K.

British Nuclear Fuels plc
Dr. R. S. Atherton
Group Manager
Environmental Protection
Risley
Warrington
Cheshire WA3 6AS
U.K.

British Petroleum plc
Dr. Peter L. Scupholme
Corporate HSE
Britannic House
1 Finsbury Circus
London EC2M 7BA
U.K.

British Telecom plc
BT Environmental Issues Unit
Dr. Chris Tuppen
Environmental Issues Manager
BT Centre
Room A245
81 Newgate Street
London EC1A 7AJ
U.K.

Brunel University*
The University of West London
Director Environmental
Management Programme
Mr. Ken Knight
Mr. Ross King
Uxbridge
Middlesex UB8 3PH
U.K.

C3E*
Professor Sylvie Faucheux
Mr. Jaques Benhaim
Université de Paris I - Panthéon
Sorbonne
Centre National de la Recherche
Scientifique
U.R.A. No. 919
Centre Pierre Mendès France
90, Rue de Tolbiac
F-75013 Paris
France

Casco Nobel A/S*
Mr. Henning Svendsen
Director of Quality Control
Mr. Anders Edgren
General Manager - Adhesives
Præstemosevej 2-4
DK-3480 Fredensborg
Denmark

Ciba-Geigy*
Mr. Michel Relave
Chef du Service Environnement
2-4 Rue Lionel Terray
B. P. 308
F-92506 Rueil Malmaison Cedex
France

De Danske Sukkerfabrikker A/S*
Mr. Steen A. Christensen
Environmental Director
Langebrogade 1
PO Box 17
DK-1411 København K
Denmark

Det Danske Stålvalseværk A/S*
Mr. Jørgen Overgaard
Technical Director
DK-3300 Frederiksværk
Denmark

Dow-Europe S.A.
Environment, Health & Safety
Ms. Paula Gasparin
Bachtobelstrasse 3
CH-8810 Horgen
Switzerland

Eco-Conseil*
Institut pour le Conseil en
Environnement
Mrs. Esther Peter-Davis
Founding President
7 Rue Goethe
F-67000 Strasbourg
France

EDF - Electricité de France
EDF Production Transport
Service Environnement
Mr. Jean-Marie Vicens
Department Manager
6 Rue Ampére
BP 114
F-93203 Saint Denis Cedex 1
France

Elf Aquitaine*
Mr. Bernard Tramier
Vice-President Environmental
Affairs
Tour Elf
Cedex 45
F-92078 Paris La Défense
France

Elf Atochem S.A.
Mr. R. Papp
Directeur Sécurité Environnement
4 cour Michelet
Cedex 42
F-92091 Paris La Défense 10
France

Elf-Sanofi*
Environment and Safety
Department
Mr. Marcel Pierre Pointet
Corporate Environment Manager
Ms. Christelle Desmarais
32-34 Rue Marbeuf
F-75008 Paris
France

European Business School
Institute for Environmental
Management and Business
Administration
Professor Ulrich Steger
Ms. Anette Anthes
Burgstrasse 4
D-65375 Oestrich-Winkel
Germany

ESEM*
Université d'Orleans
Anné Speciale Génie de
l'Environnement
Professor Michel Marchand
Rue Léonardo de Vinci
F-45067 Orleans Cedex 2
France

Fachhochschule für Wirtschaft
Pforzheim*
Professor Dr. Rudi Kurz
Coordinator of Environmental
Education
Tiefenbronner Strasse 65
D-7530 Pforzheim
Germany

Fresenius Akademie*
Mr. Matthias Willig
Akademieleiter
Hauert 9
D-44227 Dortmund
Germany

The Free University
Professor Pier Vellinga
Dr. Koen M. de Kruif
Institute for Environmental Studies
De Boelelaan 1115
1081 HV Amsterdam
The Netherlands

Georg-Simon-Ohm Fachhochschule
Nürnberg
Fachbereich Betriebswirtschaft
Professor Dr. Volker Stahlmann
Postfach 210320
D-8500 Nürnberg 21
Germany

Gesamthochschule Siegen*
Institut für Ökologische
Betriebswirtschaft e.V.
Professor Dr. Eberhard Seidel
Dr. Philipp Pott
Hölderlinstrasse 3
Postfach 101240
D-57068 Siegen
Germany

Glasuld A/S*
Ms. Jeanette Korsgaard
Environmental Officer
Østermarksvej 4
DK-6580 Vamdrup
Denmark

Groupe ESSEC*
Professor Alain Sallez
Avenue Bernard Hirsch
B.P. 105
F-95021 Cergy-Pontoise Cedex
France

Grundig AG
Ms. Cornelia von Hardenberg
Ökologie Organisation
D-90748 Fürth/Bayern
Germany

Hochschule St. Gallen
Institut für Ökologie und
Wirtschaft
Professor Dr. Thomas Dyllick
Tigerbergstrasse 2
CH-9000 St. Gallen
Switzerland

Henkel KGaA*
Umweltschutz
Dr. Klaus Kunstler
Dr. Rolf Schnakig
D-40191 Dusseldorf
Germany

Heineken Nederland B.V.
Mr. J. G. P. Twaalfhoven
Environmental Coordinator
Postbus 530
2380 BD Zoeterwoude
The Netherlands

Herberts Lacke GmbH*
Mr. Thomas May
Department AWU 248
Postfach 200854
D-42271 Wuppertal
Germany

Hoechst AG*
Dr. Hermann Teufel
Abteilung Umweltschutz
Building D. 787
D-65926 Frankfurt/Main
Germany

INSEAD*
Professor Robert U. Ayres
Sandoz Chair of Management and
the Environment
Centre for Management and
Environmental Resources
Boulevard de Constance
F-77305 Fontainebleau
Cedex
France

Institute for Applied Environmental
Economics
Mr. Marcel Crul
Grote Marktstraat 24
2511 BJ 's-Gravenhagen
The Netherlands

IBM Deutchland
Informationssysteme GmbH
Umweltschutz und Qualität
Mr. Reinhard Fasshauer
Pascalstrasse 100
D-70548 Stuttgart
Germany

IBM Europe*
Mr. Jacques Petit
Environmental Programme
Manager
Department 8140 Tour Descartes
2 Avenue Gambetta
Courbevoie
Hauts-de-Seine
Cedex 50
92066 Paris La Défense
France

IBM U.K. Ltd
Mr. Brian D. Whitaker
Environmental Affairs Manager
IBM South Bank
76 Upper Ground
London SE1 9PZ
U.K.

ICI plc*
Dr. M. Wright
ICI Group Safety
Health & Environment Department
9 Millbank
London SW1P 3JF
U.K.

International Institute for
Management Development
IMD
Dr. Francisco Szekely
Chemin de Bellerive 23
PO Box 915
CH-1001 Lausanne
Switzerland

Kingston University
Kingston Business School
Corporate Environmental Strategy
Unit
Dr. Joseph Tanega
Kingston Hill
Kingston upon Thames
Surrey KT2 7LB
U.K.

Klaus Steilmann Institut für
Innovation GmbH
Professor Dr. Wolf D. Hartmann
Feldstrasse 4
D-44867 Bochum-Wattenscheid
Germany

Kunert AG
Mr. Le Maire
Julius-Kunert-Strasse 49
D-87509 Immenstadt
Germany

Leeds Metropolitan University*
School of the Environment
Professor Peter Roberts
Brunswick Building
Leeds LS2 8BU
U.K.

Lego A/S*
Mr. Aage Hillersborg
Environmental Officer
Nordmarksvej 6
DK-7190 Billund
Denmark

London Business School
Faculty of Economics
Associate Professor Scott Barrett
Sussex Place
Regent´s Park
London NW1 4SA
U.K.

L´OREAL
Mr. Maibyrd
Directeur Environnement
41 rue Martre
F-92117 Clichy
France

Lyonnaise des Eaux Dumez,
Mr. Thierry Chambolle
Vice-president for Environment and
Technology
72 Avenue de la Liberté
F-92022 Nanterre Cedex
France

Ludwig Stocker Hofpfisterei GmbH
Mr. Friedbert Forster
Marketing
Postfach 201962
D-80019 Munchen
Germany

Linpac Plastics International Ltd
Mr. David Eggleston
Environment Manager
A1 Business Park
Knottingley
West Yorkshire WF11 0BS
U.K.

Manchester Business School*
Professor Brian Harvey
Visiting Fellow Neil Stewart
Booth Street West
Manchester M15 6PB
U.K.

Manweb plc
Mr. Michael Metcalfe
Head of Regulation
Sealand Road
Chester CH1 4LR
U.K.

Mayfair Inter-Continental
Ms. Dagmar Woodward
General Manager
Strattan Street
London W1A 2AN
U.K.

Mercedes Benz AG*
Dr. Arnulf Frisch
Produktionstechnologie und
Umwelt
Ms. Patrizia Pasquini
Umweltschutz
Werk Unterturkheim
Postfach 600202
D-70322 Stuttgart
Germany

National Power plc
Corporate Environment Unit
Ms. Sarah Hiscock
Headquarters
Windmill Business Park
Whitehill Way
Swindon
Wiltshire SN5 9NX
U.K.

NIMBAS
The Netherlands Institute for MBA
Studies
Mr. Dirk Ilsink
MBA Programme Manager
PO Box 2040
3500 GA Utrecht
The Netherlands

Nyborg-Kerteminde Business
College*
Ms. Ina Kuhlman
Mr. Jack Benzon
Ringvej 3
DK-5800 Nyborg
Denmark

The Open University
Business Development &
Marketing Office
Environmental Education and
Training
Mr. Mark Yoxon
Walton Hall
Milton Keynes MK7 6AA
Buckinghamshire
U.K.

Oxford Brookes University*
School of Planning
Professor Elisabeth Wilson
Professor Stewart Thompson
Lawn Building 304
Gipsy Lane Campus
Headington, Oxford OX3 0BP
U.K.

Powergen plc
Environmental Unit
Mr. G. W. Barrett
Environmental Adviser
Moat Lane
Solihull
West Midlands B91 2JW
U.K.

Rank Xerox Ltd
Mr. Karl Kummer
Director Environment
Parkway
Marlow
Buckinghamshire SL7 1YL
U.K.

Renlon
Mr. Richard Hall
TQ Director
148 South Park Road
Wimbledon
London SW19 8TA
U.K.

Rhône-Poulenc*
Mr. Jacques Salamitou
Directeur de l'Environnement
25 quai Paul Doumer
F-92408 Courbevoie Cedex
France

Rolls Royce plc*
Mr. Tony Jaggers
Company Environmental Manager
PO Box 31
Derby DE24 8BJ
U.K.

Roskilde University Centre*
Department of Environment,
Technology and Social Studies
Associate Professor Per H. Jespersen
Associate Professor Helge Hvid
PO Box 260
DK-4000 Roskilde
Denmark

Rover Group Ltd
Mr. Roger Twiney
Environmental Strategy Manager
Fletchamstead Highway
Cabley
Coventry CV4 9DB
U.K.

Sainsbury's
Mr. I. Samuel
Environment Affairs Manager
Stamford House
Stamford Street
London SE1 9LL
U.K.

SANU
Schweizerische Akademie für
Natur- und Umweltschutz
Ms. Gabrielle Frey
Postfach 3126
CH-2500 Biel/Bienne 3
Switzerland

Schweizerische Vereinigung für
Ökologisch bewusste
Unternehmungsführung
Dr. Arthur Braunschweig
Im Stiegen 7
CH-8134 Adliswil
Switzerland

SDA Bocconi
University of Bocconi
Professor France Amigoni
Via F. Bocconi 8
I-20136 Milano
Italy

Shanks & MacEwan PLC
Mr. Geoff Smallwood
External Affairs Manager
Woodside House
Church Road
Woburn Sands, Milton Keynes
Buckinghamshire MK17 8TA
U.K.

Shell International Petroleum
Company Limited*
Mr. Peter E. Bright
Head of Environmental Issues
Shell Centre
Freepost
London SE1 7YY
U.K.

Siemens AG
Mr. Josef Stoll
Corporate Production and Logistics
Dpt. ZPL 1 UWS
Otto-Hahn-Ring 6
D-81739 München
Germany

Southern Water PLC
Environmental Affairs
Southern House
Yeoman Road
Worthing BN13 3NX
U.K.

Sulzer - Technology Corporation
Sulzer Management Ltd
Mr. Terry Allan
Corporate Delegate Environment &
Quality
8401 Winterthur
Switzerland

Swissair
Materials Technology and
Environment
Mr. H. P. Roth
T. E. M.
CH-8058 Zürich Airport
Switzerland

Technical University of Denmark*
Institute for Product Development
Life Cycle Centre
Mr. Jørgen Jørgensen
Professor Leo Alting
Group Manager
Building 423
DK-2800 Lyngby
Denmark

Technische Universität Berlin
Fachbereich 18
Wirtschaftswissenschaften
Dr. Karin Holm-Müller
Uhlandstrasse 4-5
D-10623 Berlin
Germany

THORN EMI plc
Ms. Claire J. Baker
Public Relations Manager
4 Tenterden Street
Hanover Square
London W1A 2AY
U.K.

3M U.K. plc*
Safety Department
Dr. R. Smith
Manager Environment, Safety, Security
3M House
PO Box 1
Market Place
Bracknell
Berkshire RG12 1JU
U.K.

TopTech Studies
Drs. Petra Wassenaar
PO Box 612
2600 AP Delft
The Netherlands

United Engineering Steels Limited
Mr. R. A. Jennings
PO Box 50
Aldwarke Lane
Rotherham S60 1DW
U.K.

University of Augsburg
Kontaktstudium
Professor Dr. Bernd Wagner
Kontaktstudium Management
Eichleitnerstrasse 30
D-86159 Augsburg
Germany

University of Basel
Professor Leo Jenni PhD
Koordinationsstelle
Mensch-Gesellschaft-Umwelt
Socinstrasse 59
Postfach
CH-4002 Basel
Switzerland

University of Bradford
Management Centre
Director David Weir
Heaton Mount
Keighley Road
Bradford
West Yorkshire BD9 4JU
U.K.

University of Huddersfield*
Professor David Owen
Professor Richard Welford
Dept. of Accountancy, Law & Management
Queensgate
Huddersfield
West Yorkshire HD1 3DK
U.K.

University of Kent
Durrel Institute of Conservation and Ecology
Dr. Walter Wehrmeyer
Research Fellow
Kent Research & Development Centre
Canterbury
Kent CT2 7PD
U.K.

University of Münster
Institute for Marketing
Dr. Manfred Kirchgeorg
Universitätsstrasse 14-16
D-48143 Münster
Germany

University of Aarhus
Environmental Course
Professor Mogens Gissel
Building 135
DK-8000 Aarhus C
Denmark

University of Twente
Centre for Clean Technology and
Environmental Policy
Dr. Maarten J. Arentsen
PO Box 217
7500 AE Enschede
The Netherlands

Volkswagen AG
Umwelt, Verkehr und Forschung
Dr. Ina Thurn
Dept. 1774
Berliner Ring 2
D-38436 Wolfsburg
Germany

Wacker-Chemie GmbH
Zentralabteilung
Offentlichkeitsarbeit
Mr. Peter Hirschmann
Umweltschutz und Chemie
Hanns-Seidel-Platz 4
D-81737 Munchen
Germany

ANNEX 5

INTERVIEW GUIDE
COMPANIES

THE TEM

PROJECT No. 1

1. GENERAL INFORMATION

- Main business.

- Number of employees.

- Turnover/total assets.

- Ownership.

- R&D as a percentage of turnover or total investments.

- Environmental costs as a percentage of turnover.

- The competitive position of the company.

2. THE RESPONDENT

- Main function and organisational role.

- Educational background.

3. THE ENVIRONMENTAL SITUATION/STATUS OF THE COMPANY

General information about environmental conditions:

- What do you consider to be the most important drivers: peer pressure, environmental groups, legislation, technology, consumers, other?

- How did the greening process start in your company?

- How has your company interpreted and transformed the Brundtlandian concept of sustainable development into business policy and practice?

- How would you describe your company as regards environmental concern?

Operative functions:

- Describe the main environmental problems and concerns in your company.

- Have you achieved/are you considering environmental certification?

4. THE COMPANY APPROACH TO ENVIRONMENTAL ISSUES

Organisational initiatives:

- How are environmental problems tackled organisationally in your firm?

- Who is the key promoter/facilitator?

- The educational profile of the environment department.

- Interdepartmental conflicts.

- What are the attitudes/commitment of employees to the environmental initiatives?

- Have you designed special internal environmental incentive schemes?

Decision-making criteria and value bases:

- Describe the various environmental initiatives/strategies undertaken so far.

- Is the environmental dimension incorporated into new projects? How?

- Performance on/compliance with company-specific or general environmental standards.

- What evaluative procedures does your firm follow in prioritizing environmental initiatives? (Describe).

- Focus, objective, incentive.

5. ENVIRONMENTAL MANAGEMENT EDUCATION AND TRAINING

- Present and future environmental education requirements of employees, e.g. relating to skills, knowledge, techniques, awareness.

- Present and future multidisciplinary requirements.

- The educational profile of people involved in environmental management.

- Present and possible future issues/aspects covered in employee environmental training.

- Educational approaches in environmental training.

- What is your view of the issues/skills/knowledge taught at business schools concerning environmental management?

- What should be taught at business schools with regard to environmental management?

6. ENVIRONMENTAL COMMUNICATION AND EXTERNAL RELATIONS

Communication

- Internal communication strategies (with regard to products, processes, functional areas and employees).

- External communication strategies (with regard to products, processes, external partners in general).

The firm's external relations:

- How has your company's environmental concern affected its relations with various external partners?

7. THE FUTURE

- In general: what works well and fast at low cost (can be introduced rapidly, gives immediate results, short payback time, etc.)?

- What does not?

- How can increased strategic focus, i.e. longer time frames, and the changing context within which business is evaluated, enhance sustainability?

- What internal incentives can make sustainable business practices more likely to become a normal part of the management analysis and decision-making process?

- The future development of environmental management as a discipline and functional area.

ANNEX 6

**INTERVIEW GUIDE
INSTITUTIONS OF HIGHER EDUCATION**

1. GENERAL INFORMATION

- Purpose/scope of institution.

- Size (number of students, staff); undergraduate/graduate/postgraduate.

- Age of institution.

- Function of interviewee.

- Educational background of interviewee.

- Where/how did the "greening" of management curricula at your institution start?

- What do you consider to be the most important drivers?

2. TEACHING ACTIVITIES - ENVIRONMENTAL MANAGEMENT COURSES OFFERED

Teaching activities:

- What is offered?

- At what levels?

- Duration of each course.

- People involved.

Educational materials:

- What materials are available on different topics?

- What supporting materials exist?

- Which learning groups (undergraduate, graduate, post-graduate/executive, doctoral) are these materials intended for?

Educational strategies/teaching approaches:

- What strategies exist in each of the following three areas:
  (i) design of a subject module,
  (ii) design of an entire course;
  (iii) introduction of business-environmental issues within the institution.

- How effective are these strategies?

- What difficulties have been encountered?

- How can they best be avoided, prepared for, or overcome?

- Which additional initiatives are needed?

- Networks/practices.

3. RESEARCH ACTIVITIES

- Areas of research.

- Which areas need research?

- People involved.

- Aims of the research projects.

- Results?

- What publications or other materials are available?

- Networks/practice.

4. THE ROLE OF EDUCATIONAL INSTITUTIONS IN THE "GREENING" OF BUSINESS

What should and/or could business schools expect to accomplish?

- Essentially a proactive role?
- Essentially a reactive role?

What should educators prepare environmental management students for?

- To meet the demands of the market.
- To be effective managers of environmental resources.
- To be internal agents of change.

What must educators teach students of environmental management?

- Substantial knowledge.
- Managerial decision-making tools and methods.
- Sensitivity and awareness.
- Values and ethics.

What should attention be given to?

- Corporate environmental & resource management .
- CERM techniques or tools.
- Developing management skills in structuring roles and assignments for environmental performance, control systems and performance appraisal.

- Organisational and cultural issues which affect the implementation of policies.

How should EM be taught in order to be optimal?

- By specialist courses.
- By multidisciplinary integration.
- Is it possible for one person to master all the skills necessary?
- Where are educators to get the information they need?
- How much time should be devoted to environmental management?

5. BARRIERS

- Can corporate environmental and resource management (CERM) fit into existing institutional settings/curricula?
- Or must priorities and/or institutional settings be changed?
- Traditional perception of business curricula & business economics?
- Encountered barriers/potential barriers?

6. THE FUTURE

- Future intentions of the institution in the field of EM.
- Other future plans or changes.

ANNEX 7

MATERIAL ANALYSIS STRUCTURE NO. 1

COMPANIES

CLASSIFYING INFORMATION FROM COMPANY MATERIALS BY FUNCTIONAL AREAS

NAME OF COMPANY	
1. Values, objectives, strategies	2. Operations, production
3. Management systems, organisational structure	4. Accounting, allocation of resources, financial management
5. Human resources	6. Marketing, distribution
7. Technology and R&D	8. External relations
9. Others	

ANNEX 8

MATERIAL ANALYSIS STRUCTURE NO. 2

COMPANIES

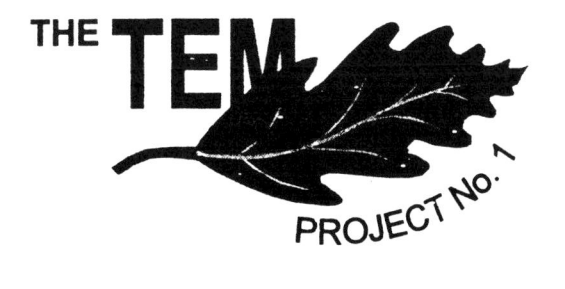

THE TEM PROJECT No. 1

TEM - ENVIRONMENTAL REPORTING QUESTIONNAIRE

Name of company: _____

TEM reg. no.: _____

Nationality of the company: **Visit:**

Austria 1   *No 1*
Belgium 2   *Yes 2*
Denmark . . . 3
France 4
Germany . . . 5
Holland 6
Italy 7
Switzerland . . 8
UK 9

Industrial sector of the company:

Consumer goods 1
Chemicals, petroleum & oil-based products 2
Electronics, appliances 3
Metal manufacturing & metal products 4
Power generation & distribution. 5
Service 6
Others 7
(Specify:_____)

A. General	*No*	*Yes*
Did the company provide a copy of its annual report ?	*1*	*2*
Did the company address specific environmental issues in its annual report ?	*1*	*2*
Did the company provide a separate environmental report ?	*1*	*2*

B. Annual report information	No	Quali-tative	Quan-titative	Both
Did the company include environmental costs:				
a. in its financial statements	1	2	3	4
b. in the notes to its financial statements	1	2	3	4
If YES, were the environmental costs included in:				
a. capital expenditures	1	2	3	4
b. site repair or restoration costs	1	2	3	4
c. contingent liabilities	1	2	3	4
d. future commitments	1	2	3	4
e. accounting policies	1	2	3	4
f. other	1	2	3	4
Did the company comment on environmental issues in its managing director's report or in any other report that the auditors have a responsibility to review?	1	2	3	4
Did the company include environmental issues elsewhere in the annual report?	1	2	3	4

C. Environmental information reported	None	Quali-tative	Quan-tita-tive	Both
Did the company provide details of an environmental policy statement (as a separate statement or incorporated throughout the report)?	1	2	3	4
Did the policy statement cover any of the following areas:				
a. air, land, and water pollution	1	2	3	4
b. natural resource conservation	1	2	3	4
c. legislative compliance	1	2	3	4
d. employee involvement	1	2	3	4
e. health and safety	1	2	3	4
f. local community issues	1	2	3	4

C. Environmental information reported	None	Quali-tative	Quan-tita-tive	Both
Did the company provide details of its future plans or specify targets for implementing its policies ?	*1*	*2*	*3*	*4*
Did these plans or targets include any of the following areas:				
a. air emissions	*1*	*2*	*3*	*4*
b. effluents	*1*	*2*	*3*	*4*
c. waste management	*1*	*2*	*3*	*4*
d. energy conservation	*1*	*2*	*3*	*4*
e. legislative compliance	*1*	*2*	*3*	*4*
f. supplier performance	*1*	*2*	*3*	*4*
g. product design	*1*	*2*	*3*	*4*
h. employee involvement	*1*	*2*	*3*	*4*
i. development and/or implementation of environmental management systems	*1*	*2*	*3*	*4*
j. environmental auditing and disclosure	*1*	*2*	*3*	*4*
k. sustainable development	*1*	*2*	*3*	*4*
Did the company report on its progress vis-à-vis previous years' targets ?	*1*	*2*	*3*	*4*
Did the company report on its environ mental performance in the following areas:				
a. air emissions	*1*	*2*	*3*	*4*
b. effluents	*1*	*2*	*3*	*4*
c. waste disposal	*1*	*2*	*3*	*4*
d. energy conservation	*1*	*2*	*3*	*4*
e. accidents and incidents	*1*	*2*	*3*	*4*
f. environmental costs, e.g. investment, fines	*1*	*2*	*3*	*4*
g. environmetal benefits, e.g. energy saving	*1*	*2*	*3*	*4*
Did the company disclose bad news as well as good ?	*1*	*2*	*3*	*4*
Where bad news was disclosed, did the company provide details of planned actions to deal with these issues ?	*1*	*2*	*3*	*4*

C. Environmental information reported	None	Qualitative	Quantitative	Both
Did the company provide details of any environmental audit carried out:				
a. internally	*1*	*2*	*3*	*4*
b. by external consultants	*1*	*2*	*3*	*4*

D. Education and training	No	Yes
Did the company disclose information about training and/or education ?	*1*	*2*
If YES, did the disclosure specify:		
a. the kind of education	*1*	*2*
b. the levels in the organisation to which it is directed	*1*	*2*
c. the educational content	*1*	*2*
d. the results of education and/or training	*1*	*2*

Completed by: _____   *Date:* _____

Comments:

ANNEX 9

MATERIAL ANALYSIS STRUCTURE

INSTITUTIONS OF HIGHER EDUCATION

ANALYSING MATERIALS FROM INSTITUTIONS OF HIGHER EDUCATION

TEACHING ACTIVITIES

SCHOOL:	
Issues	**Description in general terms**
General description - Number of environmental courses - Number of teachers engaged in environmental teaching. - How many students are enrolled - Duration - Level - Which faculty or department is active in environmental management education etc.	
Current environmental management courses - Curricula - Focus - Target group etc.	
Educational approaches - Cases - Lectures - Excursions - Reports - Company-school network etc.	
Educational materials - Type - Use etc.	

ANALYSING MATERIALS FROM INSTITUTIONS OF HIGHER EDUCATION

RESEARCH ACTIVITIES

Issues	Description
Research topics	
Aim of the research activities/projects - Main results - Expected results	
Publications available/mentioned	
Networks/collaborations	
People involved in research	

ANNEX 10

ENVIRONMENTAL COURSES OFFERED BY THE ANALYSED INSTITUTIONS OF HIGHER EDUCATION: A STRUCTURED TABULAR PRESENTATION OF THE INFORMATION IN PARAGRAPH 4.1.4

Institution No.	Country	PhD	MBA	Master	Bachelor	Other courses
1	Austria			Various environmental courses	Two environmental courses are compulsory	Seminars
2	Denmark					27-month course: theoretical + practical
3	Denmark			Experimental course in EM		
4	Denmark				Courses in LCA technique	
5	Denmark	A course in sustainable EM starts in 1994		A green MSc will start in 1994	Various courses on environmental issues	
6	Denmark	PhD programme is offered from 1995		Three environment-related courses.		

Type of education

Institution No.	Country	PhD	MBA	Master	Bachelor	Other courses
7	Denmark			One-year environmental interdisciplinary course		
8	England			New MSc starts in 1994	Six environment-related courses are offered	12 executive EM courses
9	England				Course in environmental economics	
10	England			An environmental MSc	Courses in social accounting and environmental management	
11	England		Environmental MBA with four modules			

Institu-tion No.	Country	Type of education				
		PhD	MBA	Master	Bachelor	Other courses
12	England		One course on EM			Two executive environment-related courses and 10% of another course
13	England			MSc in environmental assessment and management	Modules in environmental planning	Tailor-made training packages for companies on the EMAS.
14	England					Courses in: Corporate environmental strategy and environmental management and auditing.

Institution No.	Country	Type of education					
		PhD	MBA	Master	Bachelor	Other courses
15	England			Various environment-related courses	Various environment-related courses	Study package on environmental issues and distance learning
16	England			Various environment-related courses		
17	France			Course in environmental economics	Course in environmental economics	
18	France				Two environment-related courses	Three-day executive development programme

		Type of education				
Institu-tion No.	Country	PhD	MBA	Master	Bachelor	Other courses
19	France					One year course specialising in environmental engineering
20	France			MSc course in community planning and urban environ-mental planning		
21	Germany			1-2 day environmental courses as well as courses up to 8 months		

| Institu-tion No. | Country | Type of education |||||
		PhD	MBA	Master	Bachelor	Other courses
22	Germany			Various postgraduate conferences and workshops		3-semester course in environmental economics
23	Germany				EM is 1 of 7 possible final degree areas	
24	Germany				Specialised course in EM on the last two of eight semesters	
25	Germany				Various environmental courses - basic as well as specialised	

| Institu-tion No. | Country | Type of education |||||
		PhD	MBA	Master	Bachelor	Other courses
26	Germany			Various environmental courses		
27	Germany				Specialised course in environmental economics	
28	Switzer-land			A two-year specialised EM course		
29	Switzer-land			Various environment-related courses		

Institu-tion No.	Country	PhD	MBA	Type of education Master	Bachelor	Other courses
30	The Nether-lands		MBA degree including three environmental electives			
31	The Nether-lands			Two nine-week courses in environmental management		
32	The Nether-lands			One-year course in environment-related disciplines		
33	The Nether-lands			Three specialised environmental courses either part or full time		

European Foundation for the Improvement of Living and Working Conditions

**Training in Environmental Management – Industry and Sustainability Part 1:
Corporate Environmental and Resource Management and Educational Requirements**

Luxembourg: Office for Official Publications of the European Communities

1996 – 260 pp. – 16cm x 23.4 cm

ISBN 92-827-6927-5

Price (excluding VAT) in Luxembourg: ECU 26.50